Neil Sinyard

C000175157

Diane Kurys

MANCHESTER
UNIVERSITY PRESS

DIANA HOLMES and ROBERT INGRAM *series editors*
DUDLEY ANDREWS *series consultant*

Luc Besson   SUSAN HAYWARD

Coline Serreau   BRIGITTE ROLLET

François Truffaut   DIANA HOLMES AND ROBERT INGRAM

Agnès Varda   ALISON SMITH

forthcoming titles

Jean-Jacques Beineix   PHIL POWRIE

Bertrand Blier   SUE HARRIS

Robert Bresson   KEITH READER

Claude Chabrol   GUY AUSTIN

Jean-Luc Godard   STEVE CANNON and ELIANE MEYER

George Méliès   ELIZABETH EZRA

Jean Renoir   MARTIN O'SHAUGHNESSY

Eric Rohmer   HOWARD DAVIES

Jean Vigo   MICHAEL TEMPLE

FRENCH FILM DIRECTORS

Diane Kurys

CARRIE TARR

Manchester University Press

MANCHESTER AND NEW YORK

distributed exclusively in the USA by St. Martin's Press

Published by Manchester University Press
Oxford Road, Manchester M13 9NR, UK
and Room 400, 175 Fifth Avenue, New York, NY 10010, USA

Distributed exclusively in the USA by
St. Martin's Press, Inc., 175 Fifth Avenue, New York,
NY 10010, USA

Distributed exclusively in Canada by
UBC Press, University of British Columbia, 6344 Memorial Road,
Vancouver, BC, Canada V6T 1Z2

British Library Cataloguing-in-Publication Data
A catalogue record for this book is available from the British Library

Library of Congress Cataloging-in-Publication Data applied for

ISBN 0 7190 5094 4 *hardback*
0 7190 5095 2 *paperback*

First published 1999

05 04 03 02 01 00 99   10 9 8 7 6 5 4 3 2 1

Typeset in Scala with Meta display
by Koinonia, Manchester
Printed in Great Britain
by Biddles Ltd, Guildford and King's Lynn

Contents

List of plates

Plates 1–5 were supplied and are reproduced with permission from Diane Kurys, Alexandre Films; plates 6–9 were supplied by BFI Stills, Posters and Designs and are reproduced with permission from Sygma; plate 10 was supplied by New Light Films and is reproduced with permission from Sygma; plate 11 is reproduced with permission from New Light Films.

Series editors' foreword

To an anglophone audience, the combination of the words 'French' and 'cinema' evokes a particular kind of film: elegant and wordy, sexy but serious – an image as dependent upon national stereotypes as is that of the crudely commercial Hollywood block-buster, which is not to say that either image is without foundation. Over the past two decades, this generalised sense of a significant relationship between French identity and film has been explored in scholarly books and articles, and has entered the curriculum at university level and, in Britain, at high-school level. The study of film as art-form and (to a lesser extent) as industry, has become a popular and widespread element of French Studies, and French cinema has acquired an important place within Film Studies. Meanwhile, the growth in multi-screen and 'art-house' cinemas, together with the development of the video industry, has led to the greater availability of foreign-language films to an English-speaking audience. Responding to these developments, this series is designed for students and teachers seeking information and accessible but rigorous critical study of French cinema, and for the enthusiastic filmgoer who wants to know more.

The adoption of a director-based approach raises questions about *auteurism*. A series that categorises films not according to period or to genre (for example), but to the person who directed them, runs the risk of espousing a romantic view of film as the product of solitary inspiration. On this model, the critic's role might seem to be that of discovering continuities, revealing a necessarily coherent set of themes and motifs which correspond to the particular genius of the individual. This is not our aim: the *auteur* perspective on film, itself most clearly articulated in France in the early 1950s, will be interrogated in certain volumes of the series, and throughout, the director will be treated as one highly significant element in a complex process of film production and reception which includes socio-economic and political determinants, the work of a large and highly skilled team of artists and technicians, the mechanisms of production and distribution, and the complex and multiply determined responses of spectators.

The work of some of the directors in the series is already well known outside France, that of others is less so – the aim is both to provide informative and original English-language studies of established figures, and to extend the range of French directors known to anglophone students of cinema. We intend the series to contribute to the promotion of the formal and informal study of French films, and to the pleasure of those who watch them.

DIANA HOLMES
ROBERT INGRAM

Acknowledgements

I would like to thank Diane Kurys for twice allowing me to interview her (in October and November 1997) and for talking freely about her life and work. I would also like to thank Women In French for the opportunity of presenting some initial work on Kurys' films at the Ilkley conference in May 1996 and, similarly, the organisers of the June 1997 conference at Stirling on 'Visual Culture and French National Identity'. These conferences have given rise to two publications, 'Changing representations of women in the cinema of Diane Kurys', *Women in French Studies*, 5: Winter 1997, and 'Heritage, nostalgia and the woman's film: the case of Diane Kurys' in Sue Harris and Elizabeth Ezra (eds), *Visual Culture and French National Identity*, forthcoming, and permission to reproduce parts of this material is gratefully acknowledged. Thanks, too, to friends and colleagues who have given time to discuss work in progress.

This book is dedicated to Frank McMahon, without whose help and forbearance it would never have been written.

Introduction

Diane Kurys' first film, *Diabolo menthe* (*Peppermint Soda*), made in 1977, is dedicated to her sister 'qui m'a toujours pas rendu mon pull-over orange...'.[1] It depicts the lives of two schoolgirl sisters growing up in the early 1960s, a period which coincides with Kurys' own adolescence. Not surprisingly the film was read as thinly disguised autobiography and, in press interviews at the time of the film's release, Kurys acknowledged that the film took her personal past as its field of reference. At least three of her subsequent films have mined the same terrain for their material. *Cocktail Molotov* (1980) evokes teenage rebellion in May 1968 when Kurys herself was a student activist; *Coup de foudre* (1983) (*At First Sight*) is based on the breakdown of her parents' marriage in the 1950s; and her fifth film, *La Baule Les Pins* (1990) (*C'est la vie*), reworks the parents' separation more specifically from the point of view of the children involved.

Kurys' other three films to date have contemporary settings and are less obviously autobiographical in origin. *Un homme amoureux* (1987) (*A Man in Love*) recounts the love affair between a filmstar and a young actress who subsequently becomes a writer; *Après l'amour* (1992) (*Love After Love*) charts a year in the life of a female novelist with two lovers, each of whom has another relationship involving children; and *A la folie* (1994) (*Six Days, Six Nights*) depicts a crisis in the relationship between two adult

1 'who still hasn't returned my orange pullover'.

sisters, one of whom is an artist on the brink of commercial and critical success. Continuities between these films combined with remarks made by Kurys in interview suggest that they, too, constitute fictionalised reworkings of Kurys' own experiences. Each foregrounds an independent woman whose role as an artist caught up in triangulated relationships can be read as a stand-in for the director, herself a former actress, a screenwriter and, along with Coline Serreau, one of the most successful women directors of her generation.

Kurys herself has equivocated about the autobiographical dimension of her films, alternately denying their basis in fact and affirming her personal investment in what they represent. As she said about *A la folie*, 'Il y a certains détails vrais, mais par petites touches. Cela dit, si on creuse un peu, on se rend compte qu'on met beaucoup, beaucoup de soi, là où on croit précisément qu'on n'est pas autobiographique ... Les choses paraissent enfouies et puis elles resurgissent. Autrement'[2] (Frois 1994). Her films do not offer the spectator the 'autobiographical pact' described by Philippe Lejeune (1977), according to which an identification between the name of the author and the name of the narrator is needed to guarantee the 'truth' claims of the text. Nor do they derive from a wider totalising project on Kurys' part to document her life and the lives of those around her. They can be read as fictions without acknowledgement of their autobiographical implications or intertextual resonances. However, from that opening dedication onwards, the recurrence of characters, plot structures, incidents and emotions from one film to another prompts speculation about their autobiographical authenticity and the implied psychodrama of their author–director.

Kurys' films are of interest not just as projections of individual preoccupations but also because their focus on girls and women of the baby-boomer generation produces a symptomatic text for analysing wider issues relating to female identity and represent-

2 'Certain details are authentic, here and there. That said, if you dig a bit, you realise that you put a lot of yourself into it just when you think you're not being autobiographical ... Things seem to have been buried and then they resurface. Differently.'

ation in the latter half of the twentieth century. Yet Kurys has repeatedly refused the label of 'woman director' and sought to accommodate herself within mainstream French cinema through a personal style which aims at a wide, mixed audience. As a result, though her films inflect male-authored genres, they do not always exploit the significance of their central female roles. However, Kurys' reluctance to acknowledge gender as a factor in her filmmaking practices has not brought her recognition as an *auteur* and has not protected her from reviews which comment on her physical attributes as a woman and link certain of her films to a devalued 'feminine' sensibility by dismissing them as 'bluettes sentimentales' and 'de la guimauve'.[3] Her work needs to be understood within the specific context of French cinema and French culture, in which the concept of the *auteur*, if ostensibly ungendered, remains resolutely masculine, and in which, para-doxically, despite the growing number of women film directors, it is difficult to explore female subjectivity without subscribing to conventional patriarchal notions of French 'femininity' and sexual difference. The contradictions and compromises of her films raise the question, not just of Kurys' problematic relationship to feminism, but also of the extent to which a woman's voice can be expressed and heard within mainstream cinema in France.[4]

The commercial and critical successes of *Diabolo menthe* and *Coup de foudre*, Kurys' two most incontrovertibly women-centred films,[5] coincide with the period when the women's movement in France had its greatest impact on social and political life.[6] In the late 1970s and early 1980s, there was an audience for films by

3 'lightweight romances' and 'sentimental slush'. Recent critical attacks on Véra Belmont over *Marquise* (1997) demonstrate the prevalent misogyny among the French cinema establishment.

4 See Diana Holmes (1996), pp. 193–215 for a summary of changes in women's condition in France 1958–1994, and Ginette Vincendeau (1987), pp. 4–18, for an analysis of the problematic relationship between gender, feminism and women's filmmaking in France.

5 See Table at the beginning of the Filmography for details of the viewing figures for Kurys' films in France.

6 See Claire Duchen (1986) and Claire Laubier (1990) for further reading on women's condition in postwar France.

and about women and a significant number of French women film directors had broken into filmmaking.[7] Chantal Akerman and Marguerite Duras had foregrounded questions of 'femininity' and 'the feminine text' in *Jeanne Dielmann, 23 Quai de commerce, 1080 Bruxelles* (Akerman 1974) and *India Song* (Duras 1975) while Yannick Bellon's work had brought feminist issues to the fore in more accessible films like *La Femme de Jean* (1974). In 1977, the same year as *Diabolo menthe*, Agnès Varda released her most overtly feminist film, *L'Une chante, l'autre pas*, centred on friendship between women, and Coline Serreau's career as a director of feature films began with *Pourquoi pas?*, a challenge to conventional gender roles. When François Mitterrand came to power in 1981 at the head of a newly elected socialist government, women's issues were still very much on the social and political agenda, a situation which provides the context for the success of *Coup de foudre*. However, feminism became eclipsed later in the decade, as the economic crisis set in and the myth of 'postfeminism' became widespread (Holmes 1996: 213–15). The less overtly women-centred focus of Kurys' later films may be attributable to social changes in France and Kurys' desire to address a mainstream audience as much as to shifts in her personal preoccupations.

Female authorship and Kurys' films

While Diane Kurys may refuse the label of 'woman director' and critical theorists may argue that auteurism is an inadequate approach to understanding socially-situated, textually-produced meanings and pleasures, feminist critics and historians have argued the political necessity for defending female authorship as a useful and necessary category. If dominant male-authored cinema works to sustain the erasure, marginalisation or containment of women within a patriarchal discourse and diffuses the threat of

7 For work on French women filmmakers, see Françoise Audé (1981); Emile Breton (1984); Sandy Flitterman-Lewis (1990); Paule Lejeune (1985); Monique Martineau (1979).

sexual difference for male spectators by mediating fetishised images of the female body through a male gaze,[8] female-authored films may be more open to representations of women reworked to feminist or woman-identified ends.

Such a hypothesis is based not on the assumption of any essentialist difference between women and men, but rather on the supposition that women experience a different set of social relations and discourses which potentially inflect their literary or cinematic productions, however much their assumption of subjectivity may itself be informed by a patriarchal discourse. As Judith Mayne urges, citing Kaja Silverman, 'gendered positions of libidinal desire within the text should be read "in relation to the biological gender of the biographical author, since it is clearly not the same thing, socially or politically, for a woman to speak with a female voice as it is for a man to do so, and vice versa"' (Mayne 1990: 97). However, identifying female authorship in the cinema poses more problems than in literary criticism because of the difficulty of assuming a personal voice and because of the lack of a tradition of female authorship. While feminist film critics have become adept at deconstructing dominant male cinema, a methodology for addressing women's texts is less developed. As Mayne points out, however, the assumption of literary criticism that, 'no matter how tenuous, fractured or complicated, there is a connection between the writer's gender, personhood and her texts', can still usefully be applied to the study of female authorship in film (Mayne 1990: 90).

Feminist criticism initially devoted most attention to those women filmmakers who set out to displace the codes of dominant cinema with a radically different, alternative film practice and, as a result, as Brunsdon (1986), Quart (1988) and Colvile (1993) have argued, paid less attention to women's work within the traditions of European art cinema. Art cinema's reliance on realism and narrative, elements which make it accessible and engaging for

8 See Laura Mulvey's seminal article (Mulvey 1975), for a discussion of cinema as the site of masculine viewing pleasures. An exploration of an alternative female gaze is explored in, for example, Lorraine Gamman and Margaret Marshment (1988).

audiences, was viewed with suspicion as the vehicle for patriarchal ideology. Yet art cinema texts also allow for the expression of personal anxieties and desires, and its generic characteristics – 'subjective voice, interior realism, unresolved narrative and marked formal self-consciousness, etc.' – can be appropriated by women directors (Brunsdon 1986: 55). Since the notion of the *auteur* was developed in the 1950s by the *Cahiers du Cinéma* critics, French cinema and French film criticism have thrived on the assumption that art cinema is a vehicle for authorial self-expression. Diane Kurys' work has often been compared to that of *Cahiers* critic and New Wave director, François Truffaut, and her appropriation of filmmaking for the expression of a woman's autobiographical concerns can in itself be seen as a significant inflection of a predominantly male-centred preoccupation of contemporary European cinema.

In the course of her study of Dorothy Arzner's authorial signature, that is, the recurrent combination of aesthetic strategies and thematic preoccupations which enable a 'Dorothy Arzner film' to be identified, Judith Mayne cites Silverman's listing of the diversity of ways in which authorship can be inscribed in film, 'ranging from thematic preoccupations, to the designation of a character or group of characters as a stand-in for the author to the various enunciative strategies (sonoric as well as visual) whereby the film *auteur*'s presence is marked (whether explicitly or implicitly) to the 'fantasmatic scene' that structures an author's work' (Mayne 1990: 97). Clearly, the ways in which films articulate thematic preoccupations linked to women's experiences are important in any consideration of female authorship. Equally if not more significant are the ways in which such films address their audiences and take account of the social and psychic diversity of their female spectators. To what extent do they speak to the plurality of women's experiences by sharing knowledge about women's condition, validating skills and practices traditionally thought of as 'feminine', or contesting conventional notions of 'femininity'? Do their narratives provide pleasure and fulfilment for female spectators by privileging female subjectivity and female agency? Do they question conventional structures of looking and speaking and allow women to be subjects rather than objects of 'the look' and enjoy authoritative speech? Are sex and the body represented from female points of view? Such questions invite female-authored films to be read specifically in relation to the way they represent and invite identification with the interests and desires of women.

At the same time, given that women's cinematic production takes place within a patriarchal culture, there are problems in attributing women's actions, looks, words and desires to women authors. Women working in the mainstream need to conform to patriarchal authority and standards, even if their films also subvert them. Their anxieties about female authorship may give rise to a double voice, simultaneously muted and dominant. This concept is particularly useful in an analysis of Diane Kurys' authorial signature because of the ways in which her films both express and deny a female voice. As Maggie Humm argues, in an analogy with literary criticism, what is then required is attention to 'those minute textual places where authorial energies surface' (Humm 1997: 94).

Kurys' early films, particularly *Diabolo menthe* and *Coup de foudre*, were welcomed as women's films by feminist critics because of their overtly women-centred content and style. Barbara Quart's memories of first viewing *Diabolo menthe* are worth quoting at length:

[T]he film was a revelation after years of watching, apparently without gender consciousness, Truffaut's *400 Blows*, Menzel's *Closely Observed Trains*, Olmi's *The Sound of Trumpets*, and numerous other cherished films charting a young man's coming of age. *Peppermint Soda*'s simple existence made one notice that there were next to no films about female initiation experience; that watching young girls was a wholly different experience, moving in another and much deeper way because about oneself; and that unbelievably, through decades of film viewing one had never consciously noticed these distinctions ... [O]ne had never before seen a camera focus with this kind of attention, time, care, truth, affection and interest on young girls this way' (Quart 1988: 146).

For Marie Cardinal, *Coup de foudre* could only have been made by a woman:

> *Coup de foudre* est un film construit par un être humain de sexe féminin et un autre être humain n'aurait pas pu le faire tel qu'il est, même pas Ingmar Bergman. C'est un film différent, un tout petit peu différent. Cette toute petite différence le rend précieux, rare. Ce que voit la caméra, le temps qu'elle prend pour voir, les détails qu'elle choisit, les rythmes qui l'animent, tout ça n'est pas tout à fait comme d'habitude. Les gens qu'elle regarde ne sont pas tout à fait les mêmes que ceux qu'on nous montre ordinairement au cinéma[9] (Cardinal 1983).

Certainly, Kurys' films are unusual in their privileging of a female point of view, whether working through the problematic relationships between sisters, daughters and parents, or exploring the dilemmas of modern, independent women operating outside the norms of marriage and the family. However, their construction of femininity becomes increasingly problematic, as I have argued elsewhere (Tarr 1998), and, as already noted, Kurys herself has systematically refused the label 'woman director' and disparaged the concept of women's cinema as 'negative, dangerous and reductive' (Vincendeau 1991: 69). In 1983, she told *Le Matin Magazine* that 'les films de femmes sont mauvais pour les films, mauvais pour les femmes. Ça sent le féminisme, le cul, la guimauve'[10] (Gordon 1983). She further dismissed the idea of any specificity in women's writing in her comments on *Un homme amoureux*, 'Il y a dans le film un regard, une vision: c'est que Greta Scacchi qui joue a le statut de narratrice, ainsi je ne pense pas qu'on puisse parler encore de cette fameuse écriture féminine. A

---

9 '*Coup de foudre* is a film made by a female human being and another human being could not have made it the way it is, not even Ingmar Bergman. It's a film which is just a little bit different. This tiny difference makes it rare and precious. What the camera shows, the time it takes to show it, the details it selects, the rhythms which animate it, all these things are just a little bit different. The people it shows are not the same as the ones we normally get shown in the cinema.'

10 'Women's films are bad for films and bad for women. The term smacks of feminism, sex and schmaltz.'

ce compte-là, Truffaut était bien peu masculin et quelqu'un comme Cavani me semble bien peu féminine ...'[11] (Ferenczi 1987).

In the light of recent gender theory which insists on the fluidity and constructedness of gender positions, Kurys' signalling of 'femininity' in Truffaut's films (and elsewhere in Bergman's films and the performances of Gérard Depardieu) might be considered progressive. However, her position is accompanied by a disparagement of women which indicates an unease with her own femininity as well as mapping onto patriarchal misogynist attitudes. In a revealing interview in *Marie Claire*, she not only declared it hard to understand her mother's passionate friendship with another woman, she admitted to finding other women fundamentally banal and uninteresting because they resembled herself. 'J'ai l'impression de connaître tellement les rouages des femmes, leur psychologie, de m'identifier tellement à elles que ça m'intéresse plus d'aller vers les hommes et d'essayer de comprendre de l'autre côté'[12] (Manceaux 1983). Her reluctance to confront the diversity of ways in which women live out or challenge their femininity is confirmed by her categorisation of women into two sorts which are ultimately the same:

J'ai toujours classé les femmes en deux catégories: les hystériques qui s'accrochent et qui disent 'la dignité je m'en fous, c'est la passion qui est la plus forte. Donc je peux crier dans la rue, me battre avec lui, etc.'. Celles-là les hommes les aiment parce qu'ils ont besoin de leur hystérie: elle les rassure. Elle les renvoie à un rôle à jouer: celui de l'homme qui protège, qui calme, qui domine. Et puis les autres qui jouent les grandes dames compréhensives, dignes, nobles et qui sont plutôt les mamans. Dans [*Après l'amour*] ça donne Marianne et Lola. Le plus intéressant dans tout ça, c'est

11 'In the film there is a look, a vision: it's because Greta Scacchi, who plays in the film, has the role of narrator, but I don't think one can talk about it in terms of the famous "feminine writing". On that score, Truffaut was not very masculine and someone like Cavani doesn't seem very feminine to me.'

12 'I have the impression that I know how women work, women's psychology, and I identify with them so much that it is more interesting for me to go towards men and try to understand what's going on on their side.'

qu'on est toutes un jour des mariannes et un jour des lolas'[13] (Kurys 1992).

Given her negative attitude towards women, it is not surprising that Kurys does not set out to address a specifically female audience (she has refused to have her films shown at the Créteil International Women's Film Festival) and that in her description of the principal themes of her films – 'la famille, l'enfance, l'amour, le couple, la jalousie, la réalisation des ambitions et le renoncement à un idéal'[14] (Frois 1994) – she omits mention of their specific interest for women. It is, therefore, ironic that *Diabolo menthe* and *Coup de foudre* are her most successful films to date.

In an interview with Ginette Vincendeau in which she declared 'I am a feminist because I am a woman, I can't help it', Kurys attempted to minimise the significance of gender in her own psychological make-up. 'My point of view is different, but I don't know whether it is because I'm called Diane, because I was born a Jew, or because my parents were born in Russia, or because I'm French and I went to a particular kind of Parisian *lycée*. As well as all this, it happens that I am a woman, but that's not the main thing' (Vincendeau 1991: 70). The constant reworking in film of her traumatic childhood and its after-effects attests to her continuing need to interrogate her troubled origins and identity. The exploration of the past in Kurys' films functions, as in other autobiographical films, 'not as part of a pleasant and reassuring nostalgia trip, but in order to understand some central, often repressed, and frequently painful, memory' (Everitt 1996: 105). Kurys' films allow her to recreate her lost, painful childhood and

13 'I've always classified women in two categories: clinging hysterics who say, "I don't care about dignity, passion is more important. So it's OK to scream in the street and fight with him, etc." Men like women like that because they need their hysteria, it reassures them. It gives them a role to play, the protector who calms them down and dominates them. And then there are the others who play at being understanding, dignified and noble, and who tend to be mothers. In the film, that accounts for Marianne and Lola. But what is most interesting is that we are all mariannes one day and lolas the next.'

14 'the family, childhood, love, the couple, jealousy, achieving one's ambitions, renouncing an ideal'.

assert a measure of control over it, placing herself at the centre of stories from which she would otherwise be marginalised. As she declared herself, 'Je voulais m'imposer aux autres. Pour prendre ma revanche sur une enfance vécue difficilement à cause du divorce de mes parents. Je ressemblais à mon père et je me suis sentie rejetée par ma mère, restée seule. Il fallait que je me sente reconnue'[15] (Lejeune 1985: 159). The films' ambivalence towards women can thus be attributed in part to Kurys' identification with her father and her problematic relationship with her mother, while their sympathetic attention to childhood stems from her continuing memories of and identification with her own troubled past. Their reticences and compromises, including their reluctance to foreground the autobiographical self through a first person narrative, can be accounted for by the need to both reveal and conceal the self to gain recognition and acceptance from others. However, Kurys' inability to see her films as the work of a 'woman director' does not prevent women spectators from finding satisfactions in them nor feminist critics from seeing them as articulating the contradictions of a woman caught up in and in her own way resisting the hegemony of dominant representations of women in a patriarchal society.

Kurys' life history

Given that Kurys' films interweave fictional elements with material drawn from the author-director's personal life, a synopsis of Kurys' life history is an important intertextual reference for an appreciation of their ambivalent status as autobiographical fictions. It should be noted, however, that knowledge of Kurys' life history derives principally from the various interviews Kurys has given over the years, and that whereas she has talked freely about her childhood, adolescence and early years in the theatre, she has

15 'I wanted to impose myself on others. To get revenge for my childhood which was difficult to live through because of my parents' divorce. I resembled my father and I felt rejected by my mother and left to myself. I needed to feel recognised.'

(not surprisingly) been more reluctant to discuss details of her life since becoming a successful filmmaker. The biographical details which follow, then, which were compiled with Kurys' assistance, are necessarily partial and limited.

Diane Kurys was born in Lyons in December 1948, the younger of two sisters. Her parents were Russian Jews who had met and married in a Vichy detention camp for Jewish refugees during the German Occupation of France. Her father, a French legionnaire, saved the lives of both her mother and her mother's half-sister, who would otherwise have been deported. The breakdown of her parents' marriage in 1954 was occasioned in part by her mother's long-term friendship with another woman. As a result, the five-year-old Kurys and her sister found themselves growing up in Paris with their single-parent mother who earned a living running a women's fashion boutique, while their father ran a men's clothes shop in Lyons. Kurys' childhood and adolescence were rebellious and troubled, and at sixteen she ran away from home to join her father. When she was fifteen, she had met Alexandre Arcady, a young Jewish *pied noir* who was an activist in a leftwing Zionist youth movement.[16] In 1966, she and Arcady left France to spend a year in a kibbutz in Israel, where she witnessed the Six Day War and passed her *bac*. On her return to France, she enrolled at the Sorbonne to study literature, but became involved in the events of May 1968, after which she left university to take up a career in the theatre.

As a schoolgirl, Kurys had been fascinated by a visiting theatre company. After 1968 she worked for eight years as an actress, while Arcady also pursued a career in the theatre as an actor and director (including three years at the Jean Vilar theatre in Suresnes). Kurys first performed in a play for children called *Glomoël et les pommes de terre* and had a part in *Jarry sur la butte* with the Renaud–Barrault company in 1970. She worked with Antoine Bourseiller, among others, performed in spaces as diverse as the Café de la Gare and the Cartoucherie, and had a number of minor film and television roles. However, her life as an

16 The *pieds noirs* were French colonials born in Algeria, most of whom were forced to settle in France at the end of the Algerian war of independence.

actress was not sufficiently rewarding and she turned to adapting American plays, including *Hôtel Baltimore* by Landford Wilson, in which she acted. While in Rome for a small part in Fellini's *Casanova* (where she appears for just a few seconds), she wrote an article for *Libération* in the form of a diary of the shooting of the film. But her career as an author really began when she started writing a first-person novel about her schooldays which a friend advised her to turn into a screenplay.

The result was *Diabolo menthe*, which Kurys not only scripted but, despite her lack of previous training or experience behind the camera, was also able to direct and co-produce (as a result, she said, of her 'formidable inconscience').[17] *Diabolo menthe*'s immense success enabled her to embark on a life of writing, producing and directing. It also enabled Arcady to make his first film, the highly successful *Le Coup de Sirocco* (1979), the first of a series of films about the *pied noir* experience. The production company which Kurys and Arcady set up to produce *Diabolo menthe*, Alexandre Films, has to date (together with their second company, New Light Films, set up in 1994) produced seven films by Kurys and ten films by Arcady. Although their names may not appear on the credits for each other's films, Kurys and Arcady have a close professional relationship which means a constant sharing of ideas; Kurys is credited as co-producer of Arcady's film *Pour Sacha* (1991), which draws on their shared experiences of living on a kibbutz. In the spirit of May 1968, Kurys has never married and believes in the importance of freedom within the couple. In 1991 she and Arcady had a son, Yasha. Kurys' commitment to filmmaking has continued unabated and she is currently working on a film about the passionate relationship between George Sand and Alfred de Musset.[18]

This volume dedicates a chapter to each of Kurys' films in the order in which she made them, first because there has to date been no such detailed study of her films (critical attention has

17 'incredible foolhardiness'.
18 *Les enfants du siècle*, starring Juliette Binoche and Benoît Magimel, is due to open in May 1999.

focused primarily on *Diabolo menthe* and *Coup de foudre*), and second because the recurrence of structures and themes from film to film makes it surprisingly difficult to construct meaningful subgroups. Although Kurys' films might appear to divide easily into films set in the past and the present, the themes of *Cocktail Molotov* in particular foreshadow the themes addressed in the later films. Similarly, *A la folie* gains from being read alongside *Diabolo menthe*, since both are concerned with the representation of sisters, while *Coup de foudre* links with *Après l'amour* through the role of Isabelle Huppert who plays first, Kurys' mother, then the stand-in for Kurys herself. Kurys' most ambitious film, *Un homme amoureux*, an international co-production made primarily in English, is unique in its treatment of 'the film within the film', but needs to be read with the other films for its problematic articulation of female subjectivity.

Each chapter provides a brief contextualisation of the circumstances leading to the making of the film and its relationship to autobiographical sources, where known, analyses the film's narrative structure and use of *mise-en-scène* and sound, discusses the thematic material addressed, relates that material to Kurys' authorial presence, and assesses the film's place within contemporary French cinema. The choice of a film-by-film analysis enables the reader to follow the narrative of Kurys' development as a filmmaker, and also to read selectively in order to make particular connections between films or trace Kurys' disguised autobiographical narrative. The concluding chapter draws on these detailed textual analyses to identify the dominant elements of Diane Kurys' ambivalent authorial signature.

References

Audé, Françoise (1981), *Ciné-modèles, cinéma d'elles*, Lausanne, L'Age d'homme.
Breton, Emile (1984), *Femmes d'images*, Paris, Editions messidor.
Brunsdon, Charlotte (1986), 'Introduction' in Charlotte Brunsdon (ed), *Films for Women*, London, British Film Institute.
Cardinal, Marie (1983), 'La chambre des dames', *Le Nouvel Observateur*, 22 April.
Colvile, Georgiana (1993), 'Mais qu'est-ce qu'elles voient? Regards de Françaises à la caméra', *The French Review*, 67: 1, 73–81.

Duchen, Claire (1986), *Feminism in France from May 1968 to Mitterand*, London, Boston and Henley, Routledge & Kegan Paul.

Everitt, Wendy (ed) (1996), 'Timetravel and European film', in *European Identity in Cinema*, Exeter, Intellect Books.

Ferenczi, Aurélien (1987), 'Diane Kurys, "Mon sujet s'est construit en cours de tournage"', *Le Quotidien de Paris*, 7 May.

Flitterman-Lewis, Sandy (1990), *To Desire Differently: Feminism and the French Cinema*, Urbana and Chicago, University of Illinois Press.

Frois, Emmanuèle (1994), '*A la folie*, Diane Kurys ou l'amour vache', *Le Figaro*, 28 September.

Gamman, Lorraine and Margaret Marshment (eds) (1988), *The Female Gaze: Women as Viewers of Popular Culture*, London, The Women's Press.

Gordon, Joëlle (1983), 'Diane Kurys', *Le Matin Magazine*, 1 April.

Holmes, Diana (1996), *French Women's Writing 1848–1994*, London & Atlantic Highlands, NJ, Athlone.

Humm, Maggie (1997), *Feminism and Film*, Edinburgh University Press, Bloomington and Indianapolis, Indiana University Press.

Kurys, Diane (1992), 'Entretien avec Diane Kurys', *Après l'amour*, Publicity brochure.

Laubier, Claire (1990), *The Condition of Women in France: 1945 to the Present*, London and New York, Routledge.

Lejeune, Paule (1985), *Le Cinéma des femmes*, Paris, Editions Atlas Lherminier.

Lejeune, Philippe (1977), *Le Pacte autobiographique*, Paris, Seuil.

Manceaux, Michèle (1983), 'Diane Kurys: mon aventure-cinéma', *Marie Claire*, June.

Martineau, Monique (ed.) (1979), 'Le Cinéma au féminisme', *CinémAction*, 9 Autumn.

Mulvey, Laura (1975), 'Visual pleasure and narrative cinema', *Screen*, 16: 3, 6–18.

Mayne, Judith (1990), *The Woman at the Keyhole: Feminism and Women's Cinema*, Bloomington and Indianapolis, Indiana University Press.

Quart, Barbara Koenig (1988), *Women Directors: The Emergence of a New Cinema*, Westport, Connecticut and London, Praeger.

Tarr, Carrie (1998), 'Changing representations of women in the cinema of Diane Kurys', *Women in French Studies*, 5: 233–41.

Vincendeau, Ginette (1987), 'Women's cinema, film theory and feminism in France: reflections after the 1987 Créteil Festival', *Screen*, 28: 4.

Vincendeau, Ginette (1991), 'Like eating a lot of madeleines', *Monthly Film Bulletin*, 58, 686.

1

Diabolo menthe

Diane Kurys' entry into mainstream cinema as a successful twenty-eight-year-old film director is like a fairy story in which the princess herself overcomes the obstacles in the way of her success. Kurys had first turned to writing in the mid-1970s because of dissatisfaction with her life as an actress. She had started to write up her memories of school and adolescence, and was advised by a friend to turn her writing into a screenplay. Kurys seized on the idea with enthusiasm and submitted her original screenplay, entitled *T'occupe pas du chapeau de la gamine* (*Never Mind the Girl's Hat*), to the Centre National du Cinéma (CNC) in the hope of obtaining an *avance sur recettes* (an advance on box office receipts). In the process she was required to name the director, and since she had not thought about who might direct the film, she used her prerogative as scriptwriter to put down her own name. The script was initially turned down, but Kurys renamed it *Diabolo menthe*, made a few minor changes, resubmitted it and, in February 1977, was awarded advance funding of 500,000 francs. Determined to get the film off the ground, she then went straight to Gaumont, the biggest distribution company in France, and persuaded them to invest in the film as long as she found a producer. Eventually she discovered that Serge Laski wanted to go into feature film production and, with her partner Alexandre Arcady, she set up her own production company, Alexandre Films, to co-produce, with a total budget of 2,800,000 francs.

At that point her only experience of filmmaking, like many

women filmmakers before and after her, was from the actress' side of the camera. But she took on the role of director because the screenplay was so close to her heart, because she knew exactly what she wanted to see on screen, and because she was young and determined and blithely unaware of all that was involved. As she later admitted, '[J]'étais dans l'inconscience, je ne me rendais pas du tout compte de l'énorme aventure que ça représentait'[1] (Manceaux 1983). There followed a period of intense preparation which involved auditioning over 500 girls. Then in August, the Lycée Jules Ferry in Paris was taken over as a set (police were obliged to hold up traffic in the 18ᵉ *arrondissement* while 60s-style graffiti were painted on the walls) and Kurys embarked on her career as a director with the distinguished director of photography, Philippe Rousselot, teaching her how to handle a movie camera. Kurys acquitted herself with flying colours and so successfully managed the transition from acting to a life of writing, producing and directing.

Diabolo menthe was a huge success, well received by the majority of critics and the highest grossing French film of 1977, at one point coming second only to *Star Wars* (George Lucas 1977). It was compared with François Truffaut's *Les 400 cent coups* (1959) and Jean Vigo's *Zéro de conduite* (1933) and awarded the Prix Delluc[2] (by eight votes to seven for Pierre Schoendorffer's *Le Crabe-tambour*), though some cinemas were reluctant to advertise the fact since it might make the film seem too 'arty' for a popular audience. Yet the centring of *Diabolo menthe* on the point of view of two young girls broke with the male-centred focus of mainstream popular cinema, and directly addressed the memories and experiences of its female spectators, building on the concern with women's issues which emerged in the aftermath of May 1968. Kurys wanted her everyday story of two rebellious young girls growing up in the 1960s to stimulate critical reflection on the

1 'I was foolhardy, I had no idea what an enormous venture it would be.'
2 Kurys was the youngest director ever to receive this award, which had been awarded before her to directors like Jean Renoir, Marcel Carné, Jean Cocteau, Henri-Georges Clouzot and Jacques Tati. In 1996, it was awarded to Sandrine Veysset for *Y aura-t-il de la neige à Noël?*, another first film with autobiographical resonances by a woman director.

significance of the period, 'J'avais envie de porter un regard
critique sur les rapports parents-enfants, le pouvoir du lycée, les
filles entre elles...'[3] (Kurys 1978: 19). The title *Diabolo menthe* was
intended to evoke the image of young French teenage girls, who
drank peppermint soda because they did not know what they
wanted and indeed, according to Kurys, did not know much about
anything (Kurys 1977). The film does not venture into experiment-
ation with film form, but neither does it derive its style from the
popular genres, tightly plotted narratives and star-led casts
characteristic of mainstream cinema.[4] As Kurys pointed out, 'il n
y'a pas d'action, pas de vedettes, pas de violence, pas de cul, pas de
fric'[5] (Kurys 1978: 19). Instead, despite its precisely delineated
early 1960s setting and atmosphere, it offers spectators of all ages,
male and female, an unsentimentalised, instantly recognisable
depiction of the pains and pleasures of being young.

Though *Diabolo menthe* is ostensibly set during the 1963 school
year, the film is an amalgam of Kurys' memories from the years
1960 to 1965 of herself and her sister growing up as 'latchkey
kids' in a single-parent family, a situation which at the time was
relatively unconventional. *Diabolo menthe*'s opening dedication to
Kurys' sister establishes Kurys' authorial presence and an
autobiographical perspective on the events of the film, inviting the
spectator to understand that thirteen-year-old Anne Weber
(Eléonore Klarwein) will grow up to be Diane, the filmmaker.
However, though the spectator is invited to sympathise with
Anne's point of view throughout the greater part of the text, the
point of view of the older sister, fifteen-year-old Frédérique (Odile
Michel) is also privileged, particularly in the second half of the
film. Kurys has admitted that, though Anne is 'me completely',
Frédérique is inspired both by her sister and by 'myself some-
times' (Murray 1980). The foregrounding of both girls allows
different stages in Kurys' life to be dramatised in the same film as

3 'I wanted to take a critical look at parent–child relationships, the power of the
   lycée, girls together ...'
4 See Susan Hayward (1993) for a detailed analysis of developments in French
   cinema through the 1970s and 1980s.
5 'there's no action, no stars, no violence, no sex, no money'.

well as representing complicities and rivalries between sisters (a relationship Kurys was to turn to again in *La Baule Les Pins* and *A la folie*). In interviews held when the film opened, Kurys talked freely about her unhappy childhood following the break-up of her parents' marriage, and her rebellious adolescence. The film draws not just on her family background but on her suffering at the hands of authoritarian school teachers, her fear and ignorance about sex, her sister's involvement in the peace movement, and the loss of a girlfriend. *Diabolo menthe*, then, is not just a document of the times or an exercise in nostalgia. Its critical purchase on the period can be read on a personal level as a way of exorcising the traumas of childhood and adolescence, while on a more general level it works to inscribe what was happening to girls into representations of French society in the 1960s.

The film's structure is not based on the build-up to a dramatic climax typical of classic narrative. Instead its cyclical structure is linked to the academic year, beginning and ending on the beach where the girls spend the summer holidays with their father, with the ordering of events determined by chronology rather than plot. In *des femmes en mouvement*, Kurys refers to her desire to create 'une sorte de tableau impressioniste avec les mille composantes de la vie d'une adolescente en 63'[6] (Kurys 1978: 19). More important than the linear plot are the ups and downs in the emotions experienced by the two sisters, which are constructed through a series of brief but precisely delineated scenes, 'a series of oscillations, which are sensitive to slight shifts in mood' (Foster 1995: 211). These scenes deal with the substance of everyday life, minor crises taking place at home and at school rather than major melodramas. But they are perceived through the eyes of the girls and express the rebelliousness produced by the often unjustified and unjustifiable attempts to impose discipline within the home and the *lycée*. Together they trace crucial phases in Anne and Frédérique's growing up and build up a complex picture of the sisters' relationships with each other and with their parents, teachers and friends. The 'inbetweenness' of the period is

6 'a sort of impressionist painting of the thousand components in the life of an adolescent girl in 1963'.

captured structurally by the opposition between term time, when the girls live with their mother (Anouk Ferjac) in Paris, and the holidays spent on the beach or in the mountains, which are associated with the father (Michel Puterflam) or Frédérique's boyfriend Marc (Darius Depoléon). The narrative is framed by scenes on a beach in Normandy and punctuated by a skiing holiday at Christmas and Frédérique's camping holiday with Marc at Easter, scenes which are rendered through the incorporation of a montage of photographs. This device economically figures the passing of time but also emphasises the structuring opposition between the world of the father and the world of the mother, a mark of Kurys' authorial signature, which is reinforced rather than resolved by the film's cyclical ending.

Anne's narrative strand encompasses a number of different but interrelated threads, including her difficult relationship with both her mother and her father, her longing to grow up and be like her sister and her poor performance at school which, along with other signs of antisocial behaviour, mark her as a child who is both vulnerable and defiant. Her first words, 'J'ai pas envie ... Je m'en fous!',[7] are indicative of the sullen attitude she displays throughout much of the film. She argues with her mother about everything, from pocket money, to taking the bus to school, to wearing stockings instead of socks; while her communication with her father is limited to asking him for things, like a cheque for her mother and a holiday at L'Alpe d'Huez. She expresses her envy of Frédérique by stealing a holiday snap of her boyfriend and constantly trying to hang around with Frédérique and her girlfriends, and she cries when she realises Frédérique doesn't love Marc any more. She longs to start menstruating and goes to some lengths to disguise the fact that her periods have not started, stealing a sanitary towel from her sister and pretending to have to go to the toilet in the middle of a class. At school she has lively conversations with Martine and Sylvie in the school courtyard and rebels against the ineffective and authoritarian teachers in the classroom; but she also cheats at and fails her schoolwork and lies

7 'I don't want to ... I don't give a damn!'

to her mother about the reason for her low marks. When Frédérique's friend Muriel runs away from home, Anne mischievously makes an anonymous phone call pretending to have news of her; later she gets caught shoplifting just after her mother has bought her a new dress. The end of the school year brings no resolution to the pains of growing up, but it reconciles the sisters who turn their backs on the end-of-year school dance together before being despatched on their summer holidays.

Anne's close but fraught relationship with Frédérique is established from the beginning of the diegesis by the alternation between shots of Anne in isolation and the use of two-shots, as in the railway carriage when they giggle at the faces of their fellow passengers. Frédérique is capable of being solicitous about Anne's welfare, taking her on an illicit trip to the cinema to see *The Great Escape*, with Steve McQueen, for example, or leaving the bedroom door open so that she can continue to see what is happening in the other room. But Frédérique also exercises her authority as elder sister, as when she stops Anne having a peppermint soda in the local café (so justifying the film's title) or when she punishes Anne for misbehaving. A studious pupil, Frédérique's initially complicit relationship with the mother becomes problematic as she becomes older and more independent. She gets into trouble for returning home from a party after the agreed time, and for receiving love letters from Marc which the mother feels are not appropriate for her age (and which she is forced to destroy). She is also told off for her political activities, and reacts stubbornly by collecting money for the peace movement, taking part in a demonstration and facing punishment at school. As a result, she loses her best friend, Perrine, whose bourgeois parents deplore girls getting involved in politics. However, she befriends the fascinating new girl, Muriel, whose mother committed suicide and who runs away with her boyfriend, deciding that freedom is more important than school; and another friendship begins with Pascale, a classmate who witnessed the Charonne massacre[8] and

8 On 8 February 1962, outside the Charonne metro station, police charged a peaceful demonstration against the OAS (Organisation de l'armée secrète), resulting in the deaths of nine demonstrators.

who acts opposite her in the end-of-year school play. The film follows the development of Frédérique's awakening sexuality through her unsatisfactory relationship with Marc, her crush on Muriel's father and her awareness of a current of desire between herself and Pascale which she chooses not to act on. Despite her growing distance from family and school, Frédérique's role culminates in a starring part in the school production of Molière's *Les Femmes savantes*, an event which is attended by both her mother and her father. The recourse to creativity and self-expression as a way of dealing with unhappiness in personal relationships is a theme which recurs throughout Kurys' work.

The narratives of teenage girls' experiences in the 1960s are authenticated through precise attention to the period detail of setting, props, costumes and music. The décor of the Lycée Jules Ferry (Kurys' old school), with its imposing gates and railings, its high ceilings, its echoing corridors and its lack of intimacy, reproduces the authoritarian atmosphere of the 1960s and contrasts with the spontaneity of the girls' behaviour which the school authorities try to repress. Kurys felt that the *lycée* was the main protagonist of the film, 'Il est magnifique, l'architecture, les fresques, les couleurs, la peinture, cette sorte de beige rose, formaient vraiment un décor qui parlait: on sentait bien toute la contradiction entre un univers oppressant, la difficulté qu'on a à grandir et en même temps la beauté de la jeunesse'[9] (Manceaux 1983). The oppressiveness of the school setting is mirrored in the drab, desexualising uniforms worn by the girls and the rules and regulations about the girls' appearances which deny individuality and which the girls resist in every way possible. Their outbursts of rebellion contrast with the conformism of the assorted school-teachers, many of whom are cast as though from the girls' point of view as grotesque caricatures, like the drably dressed maths teacher who cannot keep discipline (Dominique Lavanant), the exotic but hopelessly unfit sports teacher (Dora Doll), the English

9 'It's magnificent. Its architecture, frescoes, colours, that sort of pinkish-beige paintwork, produced a décor which really said something. You can feel the contradiction between an oppressive universe, the difficulty of growing up, and at the same time the beauty of youth.'

teacher whose pronunciation of English leaves much to be desired (Marthe Villalonga).

Costumes, then, are not just a mark of period authenticity, they are also a source of tension within the text, as in Anne's insistent desire to wear stockings, and the sadistic art teacher's determination to wipe off a girl's eye make-up and scrape off her nail varnish, witnessed by Anne and Martine. Outside of school, the girls' dresses and boys' suits, their hairstyles and dancing styles, are shown off to particular effect in the scene of the *surprise-party*[10] and the film also takes pleasure in recreating 1960s beachwear, handbags and summer frocks, drawing on 'feminine' spectatorial pleasures which Kurys was to develop later in *Coup de foudre* and *La Baule Les Pins*. The brief scene in which the mother, who works in a boutique called Magdalena (the name of Léna's boutique in *Coup de foudre*), sets out to purchase dresses for her daughters from a wholesaler is typical of Kurys' economical use of *mise-en-scène*. The racks of period clothing serve as a realistic backdrop to the development of the characters and their interactions. The scene combines the mother's concern for her daughters' appearance and need as a single parent to be careful with money with a demonstration of her role in the rag trade and her ability to charm men. At the same time it contrasts Anne's unselfconscious pleasure in her developing body with Frédérique's awareness of the male wholesaler's potentially threatening gaze, a gaze which makes her refuse to try on any clothes. The scene's final focus on Frédérique's look allows the spectator to share her resistance to male dominance and become uncomfortably aware that feminine pleasures in fashion have a problematic relationship with a male-controlled fashion industry. It raises the critical question of who looks and who is looked at, echoing the scene when the girls themselves look at the would-be voyeurs hovering on the other side of the school railings.

10 *Diabolo menthe* could have been the model for the recent series of television films commissioned by Arte under the umbrella title *Tous les garçons et les filles de mon âge*, in which filmmakers addressed the problems of growing up at various moments in postwar France, and were required to include a scene at a party.

The soundtrack too works to authenticate the period reconstruction. It draws on the popular culture of the period, mixing in
radio programmes like 'Salut les Copains' and songs by the likes
of Johnny Halliday, Claude Nougaro, Sylvie Vartan and Cliff
Richard, whose 'Living Doll' accompanies the opening credit
sequence. It is also marked by the clamour of the school, particularly the school bell. But it is dominated by the voices of the
young girls. As a schoolgirl spectator points out, 'Dans un lycée de
filles, on peut se parler, on se parle, il y a une proximité entre
nous'[11] (Quatre lycéennes 1978: 19). In *Diabolo menthe*, the camera
constantly centres on the girls anxiously discussing everything
from the barbarities of the teachers to boys and the white slave
trade. The language of the younger girls reveals their sexual
naïvety: Sylvie considers that she has slept with a boy because they
lay down on a bed together, and thinks that men's penises grow to
two metres in length. (Some reviewers felt that Kurys should have
inserted corrections to the wilder surmises of her protagonists.)
But girls' voices also relay what is happening in the world, and
register protests. Anne reports hearing the news of Kennedy's
death on the radio, Frédérique tells her mother about the rise of
anti-Semitic groups at school. In the course of a history lesson,
Pascale describes the police violence she saw from her balcony at
the time of the Charonne demonstration and also the funeral of
the victims, one of whom was a fifteen-year-old schoolboy. Muriel
protests about the petty restrictions of school life by screaming, 'Je
vous dis merde!'[12] over and over again, whirling around in the
school courtyard, her voice and movement shattering the order
and symmetry of the school. The sympathetic attention to girls'
words and voices and the range of registers with which they are
entrusted is one of the film's principal cinematic innovations.

Kurys carefully embeds other political references within the
film. As the school year begins, so a tearful *pied noir* girl finds
herself alone in the courtyard without a class to go to, and the
ignorant school administrator thinks (rather improbably) that
Oran, where she comes from, must be a private school. When the

11 'In a girls' school, we can talk to each other and we do, we're close to each other.'
12 'Shit on you!'

girls put 'My Yiddish mama' on the record player to celebrate their mother's birthday, the film suggests that the Jewish heritage of the Weber girls is taken for granted, and when Frédérique refers to anti-Semitism at school, her outburst appears to be a way of attacking her mother, since she has not actually been the victim of racial abuse. But at the end of the school year, Frédérique is involved in a clash outside the school gates between a Fascist anti-Semitic group and those protesting in favour of the peace movement. The film is thus aware of issues raised by race and difference which are hinted at rather than insisted on.[13] It constructs a mosaic of notations which may or may not set up resonances in the individual spectator, but makes the film available for a reading of the girls' rebellion against the background of the more general social unrest of the period. Not only are politics seen to be as much of a taboo area as sex in the eyes of the authorities, the inclusion of political references allows the girls' experiences, too, to be seen as a significant element of contemporary French history.

Quart (1988) notes how both girls are more rebellious than one might notice on first viewing the film, and the film uses their rebelliousness to make links with the beginnings of the sexual revolution of the 1960s and the revolt against the repressive authority of parents and teachers which was to culminate in the events of May 1968. As Kurys has pointed out, the eighteen-year-olds of 1968 were thirteen in 1963. Sexual revolution is figured in particular through the character of Muriel, who runs away from school to live out a romantic idyll with her boyfriend and demands the right to sexual freedom. Revolt within the family is expressed through the girls' reactions to their mother's unjust and irrational rules and regulations, her intrusion into their privacy, her lack of respect for their individual thoughts or their need for financial autonomy, her reluctance, in other words, to let them grow up.

13 Other women's films addressing issues raised by ethnicity and difference include Charlotte Silvéra's semi-autobiographical *Louise l'insoumise* (1984), which addresses the difficulties of integration experienced by a young Jewish Tunisian girl, and Martine Dugowson's *Mina Tannenbaum* (1993), which explores in depth the effects of a Jewish heritage on two young women friends.

Revolt at school is traced through the girls' collective rebellion against those incompetent or abusive teachers and administrators who use their power to stultify the girls rather than stretch their minds (the history teacher providing an honourable exception). The film critiques the way the girls are treated and implicitly pleads for a more liberated and imaginative form of education which would take account of their needs and interests. But revolt is also linked to a wider protest about the Gaullist society of the 1960s which, beneath its complacent surface, supported the development of nuclear weapons and allowed the growth of terrorist, Fascist and anti-Semitic factions.

The narrative structure, *mise-en-scène* and soundtrack, with their references to the actuality of the 1960s, work together in *Diabolo menthe* to construct a believable world which rekindles anger at the constraints of the period as much as it evokes nostalgia for the past. Yet nostalgia, or some sort of emotional identification with the girls' recognisable 'growing pains', is also encouraged, in particular by the use of incidental music, which starts up with the girls' first day back at school. The music invites a sympathetic, if not sentimental response to certain scenes: Anne's theft of the photograph of Frédérique's boyfriend, getting a 'sick note' to avoid a maths test, wearing stockings for the first time, and waiting awkwardly on the station platform with a boy she met at her first party; Frédérique's rejection of Marc after their unhappy camping trip, her feelings after kissing Muriel's father, and her discovery but refusal of desire between herself and Pascale during the school outing to the Abbaye de Port Royal. These moments enable the spectator to look back with affection on the girls' awakening sexuality and rites of passage, with their attendant feelings of anxiety, jealousy, ignorance, fear and excitement. The delicacy of the way the issues are handled from the girls' points of view can be usefully compared with the ways girls are usually constructed within a male-centred scenario in dominant French cinema.[14] At the same time, the sentimental song by Yves Simon which accompanies the closing credit

---

14 See for example Ginette Vincendeau (1992).

sequence suggests that a male voice is needed to validate those experiences.

The element of nostalgia indicates that, in addition to its documentation of everyday life in the 1960s, *Diabolo menthe* sets in play a psychodrama based on the dynamics of the dysfunctional family, which is developed further in Kurys' later films. The parents' separation sets up a tension between the distant world of the father and the close but often oppressive world of the mother, at the centre of which is the defiant, insecure younger daughter, who is constantly looking for ways to make her mother and father aware of her presence. Anne is regularly framed in isolation from the rest of her family, be it on the beach when she refuses to go swimming with her sister, at a family picnic when she refuses to let her mother's boyfriend take her photo, or at the end when the shot of her walking towards the sea alone is followed by a freeze-frame in which she turns back to face the camera. At three different moments, two-shots of the mother and Frédérique on the bed are intercut with shots of Anne looking on at them, twice from the interior of her darkened bedroom, once framed against the doorway. The two-shots signal Frédérique's privileged relationship with the mother, while Anne is neither integrated into the scene nor able to exist outside of it. If Anne longs to replace her sister in the warmth of the mother's embrace, the film does not allow that desire to be achieved. Shots like those of the lonely onlooker constitute a key element of Kurys' authorial signature.

The film privileges the girls' relationship with their mother, a theme which normally constitutes a structuring absence in dominant French cinema (and cinema more generally). The sympathetic representation of a woman who is also a mother leading a free and independent life is a rare phenomenon. In *Diabolo menthe*, Mme Weber is represented realistically trying to cope with holding down a job, bringing up two children, psoriasis, not much money, a husband who does not pay his share of the expenses on time, and a boyfriend whom she has to keep secret from her husband so as not to prejudice her divorce. She is a strong and attractive woman who is also embattled and vulnerable, as signalled in particular by the brief scene when she telephones her unseen friend, Cécile, to express her anxieties about her health (a hint of the theme of friendship and support between women which forms the subject matter of *Coup de foudre*). But Mme Weber, as seen through the eyes of her daughters, does not escape criticism. Despite her physical affection and her concern about their academic progress, she leaves them to return home to an empty flat, favours one daughter over the other, and abuses her maternal authority by the way she polices their activities. Typically, she responds to Anne's first period by slapping her face 'to give her cheeks colour for the rest of her life', a response (apparently traditional in Kurys' family) which reduces Anne to tears, so that the hug which follows comes too late to repair the psychological damage. The scene highlights the problematic of the daughter's desire both to be united with and separated from the mother, and Mme Weber emerges from the film as a controlling, phallic figure who can neither give her daughters the love they need nor allow them to grow up and separate from her. As a result, she increasingly loses intimacy with and control over her children, who are far from being the obedient model daughters she had wanted. In *Diabolo menthe*, then, the mother figure is the ambivalent repository of both love and resentment.

Attitudes to the father are also ambivalent. Whereas the mother is part of the girls' everyday life, the father's sporadic presence linked to holidays and special occasions means that the masculine world appears distant and other, 'C'est un film rempli de bonnes femmes; peu d'hommes, car l'homme représente l'interdit, la curiosité, le tabou surtout pour ces petites minettes en herbe, en uniforme beige'[15] (Petit-Castelli 1977). The sense of otherness is borne out by the film's fetishisation of the male figure through the photograph of Marc, Frédérique's boyfriend, which Anne steals and keeps hidden away in her purse, and by the conversations of the young schoolgirls which demonstrate the fascination exercised by boys on the female imagination. But in reality the male characters do not live up to female expectations.

15 'The film is full of women; there are hardly any men, because men represent the forbidden, curiosity, the taboo, for these growing girls in their beige uniforms.'

The father is an embarrassment to his daughters as he waves goodbye at the railway station after the summer holiday. Seen from the girls' point of view in a downward-angle shot, he is balding, poorly dressed, speaks in an unusually high voice and has to be reminded about the maintenance cheque he owes. Similarly, when he meets them unexpectedly after school to take them out to a restaurant, he is unable to communicate his tenderness and, under their critical scrutiny, makes do with telling a very bad joke and ordering them to eat their food before it gets cold; though he comes to see Frédérique perform in the school play, he is too timid to stay around and talk to his daughters afterwards. The play of absence and presence in relation to the father is replicated by the role of the briefly glimpsed Marc. Absent, his photos and letters provide fodder for the female imagination; present, despite being a nice-looking, nice-mannered youth, he simply gets on Frédérique's nerves. Frédérique's subsequent fascination with Muriel's widower father looks like a displacement of desire for her own absent, inadequate father. Present (an architect who works at home) and nurturing (he looks after Muriel single-handedly), he is also a lonely and vulnerable man; but he is unable to give Frédérique what she wants, and his gentle resistance to her advances does not prevent her from shedding a tear.

Diabolo menthe's concern with image and representation appears to be closely connected with the masculine, but its function is more ambivalent than that. In the opening shot, a holiday snap of the two sisters and Marc taken by a male photographer is a trick shot in which Frédérique's upright head is juxtaposed for the camera with Marc's recumbent body. The active agent in the making of this image is given as male, a motif repeated later in the film through the role of the mother's boyfriend, Philippe, as a photographer. But control over the image is also vested in the girl who (it is assumed) organised its *mise-en-scène* and uses it humorously, if awkwardly, to call gender roles into question by taking on a mix of feminine and masculine features. Frédérique's role in *Les Femmes savantes* has a similar function. Not only does her performance allow her the narcissistic pleasure of being looked at, it also permits her to dress up as a man with a moustache and take on an active, desiring masculine role. The world of representation, then, be it photography or theatre, allows the adolescent girl to cross borders and express the fundamental fluidity of gendered positions. At the same time, Anne's most treasured photograph is not the one of Marc but the one which represents her parents as a couple, the object of nostalgia, loss and melancholy. The film thus hints at the complex and contradictory desires underlying the drive to become an image-maker: the desire to represent the self in a way which transcends everyday constraints by fusing masculine and feminine characteristics; the desire to objectify and fix the desired male other; and the more problematic, potentially regressive desire to recreate and possess in representation the imaginary, lost nuclear family.

Kurys' first film offers a subtle challenge to dominant cinematic representations by the way it both pays homage to and cocks a snook at some of the male-authored classics of French cinema. Its debt to *Zéro de conduite* is clear from the girls' defiance of their teachers, in particular Muriel's resounding and repeated echoing of 'Je vous dis merde!', an act which puts girls at the centre of a narrative of rebellion. The references to *Les 400 coups* are multiple, including the circulation of images in school (Anne's treasured photos replacing Antoine Doinel's pin-up), the pupils getting ink all over their fingers, the problematic relationship with the mother, the illicit trip to the cinema, Anne's stealing and Muriel's running away from home. In particular, Kurys reworks the final freeze-frame of *Les 400 coups* which ends on a close-up of Doinel turning back from the sea. Her substitution of a freeze-frame of Anne's face reclaims a place for feminine viewing pleasures in French film culture, as does her incorporation of filmic references in the girls' conversations and activities. Though they talk about Alain Resnais' *Muriel* (1963) (a New Wave film which critiques the French presence in Algeria), they go off to see Steve McQueen in *The Great Escape* (John Sturges 1963) and look forward to seeing Cliff Richard in *Summer Holiday* (Peter Yates 1962).

Diabolo menthe also makes an important contribution to the semi-autobiographical film which fictionalises the filmmaker's autobiographical past, particularly her/his childhood. Such an approach has proved popular amongst both male and female filmmakers, as in Jean-Loup Hubert's *Le Grand chemin* (1987), Louis Malle's *Au revoir les enfants* (1987) and André Téchiné's *Les Roseaux sauvages* (1994), but also Véra Belmont's *Rouge Baiser* (1985), Claire Denis' *Chocolat* (1988) and Marie-France Pisier's *Le Bal du gouverneur* (1990). In all these cases, nostalgia for the past is combined with an exploration of the permeability of the individual and the social which challenges the visual pleasures of period reconstruction and, to varying degrees, interrogates not just family life but French society in general. The real achievement of *Diabolo menthe* is its inscription into the national narrative of a 'feminine' universe seen from female points of view.

References

Foster, Gwendolyn Audrey (1995), *Women Film Directors: An Introductory Bio-Critical Dictionary*, New York, Greenwood Press.

Hayward, Susan (1993), *French National Cinema*, London and New York, Routledge.

Kurys, Diane (1977), '*Diabolo menthe*', *Cinéma Français*, 18.

Kurys, Diane (1978), 'Entretien avec Diane Kurys', *des femmes en mouvement hebdo*, 2 February.

Manceaux, Michèle (1983), 'Diane Kurys: mon aventure-cinéma', *Marie Claire*, June.

Murray, Scott (1980), 'Diane Kurys', *Cinema Papers*, August–September.

Petit-Castelli, Claude (1977), '*Diabolo menthe*', *Le Matin*, 22 September.

Quart, Barbara Koenig (1988), *Women Directors: The Emergence of a New Cinema*, Westport, Connecticut and London, Praeger.

Quatre lycéennes (1978), 'A propos de *Diabolo menthe*', *des femmes en mouvement hebdo*, 2: 18–19, 2 February.

Vincendeau, Ginette (1992), 'Family plots: the father and daughters of French cinema', *Sight and Sound*, 1: 11, 14–17.

facing

1 The sisters on holiday with their father (Michel Puterflam) in Normandy in *Diabolo menthe,* 1977

2 Anne and schoolfriends in *Diabolo menthe,* 1977

3 Frédérique (Odile Michel) and her mother (Anouk Ferjac) in *Diabolo menthe,* 1977

facing

4 The graffiti-sprayed Citroën DS of *Cocktail Molotov*, 1980

5 Anne (Elise Caron), Bruno (François Cluzet) and Fred (Philippe Lebas) in Venice in *Cocktail Molotov*, 1980

6 Léna (Isabelle Huppert) and Madeleine (Miou-Miou) look for Sophie in *Coup de foudre*, 1983

7 Jane (Greta Scacchi) and Steve (Peter Coyote) meet outside the Cinecittà Studios in *Un homme amoureux*, 1987

8 Léna (Nathalie Baye) consoles her daughters in *La Baule Les Pins*, 1990

9 Lola (Isabelle Huppert) and David (Bernard Giraudeau) confront each other in *Après l'amour*, 1992

10 Franck (Patrick Aurignac), Alice (Anne Parillaud) and Elsa (Béatrice Dalle) in *A la folie*, 1994

11 Diane Kurys at the time of *A la folie*, 1994

2

Cocktail Molotov

After the success of *Diabolo menthe*, Kurys was inundated with
proposals for a second film and invited to write a script about the
Club Méditerranée for Columbia Studios. However, she soon
decided that she preferred her independence and her next
screenplay constitutes a companion piece to *Diabolo menthe*. As
Kurys remarked, 'J'avais l'impression d'avoir encore des choses à
raconter: alors je me suis lancée encore une fois toute seule et j'ai
écrit la suite: ce qui arrive aux filles de 18 et 20 ans. Et puis, il me
paraissait urgent de raconter la période de 68 parce qu'en 78 il y a
eu une sorte d'enterrement en grande pompe de Mai 68'[1]
(Lejeune 1987: 159). The choice of May 1968 as a setting provided
the opportunity for investigating yet again the links between a
particular historical moment and personal memories of repression and revolt, in this case the revolt of a seventeen-year-old
girl which takes place in parallel to the events of May.

    Cocktail Molotov was funded in part by the television channel
Antenne 2, but Kurys produced the film herself, both to retain her
independence and because of delays in receiving payment for
Diabolo menthe. She found herself responsible for a budget of
6,500,000 francs and forced to rethink her screenplay since there
was insufficient money for reconstructions of the student

---

1 'I felt I still had things to say; so I started writing again, on my own, and wrote
the follow-up: what happens to girls of eighteen and twenty. Also, I thought it
was crucial to describe the period of 1968 because in 1978 there was a sort of
ceremonial burial of May 68.'

barricades in the streets of Paris. She cast two drama students,
Elise Caron and Philippe Lebas, in the leading roles, along with
the then relatively unknown François Cluzet whom she had seen
acting in Genet's *Haute Surveillance*. Two months of shooting on
location in Venice, Nice, Lyons and Paris followed, with Philippe
Rousselot once more as director of photography. At the editing
stage Kurys reinforced the personal drama by cutting out two
specifically political sequences, the demonstration outside the
Renault factory at Flins (which the film was due to end with) and a
meeting of political activists in Italy. The film opened in February
1980 to a lukewarm reception, which may be accounted for in part
by the mismatch between the personal dramas and the historical
moment. Kurys' concern with May 1968 is rooted in her own
experience, 'Mai 68, pour moi, c'est le résultat de notre enfance, la
conséquence logique de nos treize ans brimés, tristes, solitaires:
entre les deux, il ne s'est rien passé ...'[2] (Rouchy 1980). However,
though her own adolescence led to her becoming a student
activist, in *Cocktail Molotov* she focuses on a trio of teenagers who
miss out on what was going on. The film thus fails to deliver the
dramatic purchase on the events promised by the title, and is
informed as much by Kurys' later disillusion with May as by the
enthusiasms of the period, 'On croyait pouvoir changer le monde,
les habitudes de pensée. On militait ou pas. Puis l'essence est
revenue; tout est rentré dans l'ordre. Ce qui n'était qu'une
révolution bourgeoise a avorté'[3] (Wachthausen 1980). Despite its
relative failure, however, the film is particularly interesting for the
way it articulates May 1968 with female experience and the
personal psychodrama typical of a Kurys film. The film's focus on
'la révolte et le premier amour' of its female protagonist is clearly
out of phase with more male-centred narratives of the events of
May.

2 'May 68 was the result of our childhood, the logical consequence of being
repressed, sad, solitary thirteen-year-olds; between the two [dates], nothing
happened ...'
3 'We thought we could change the world, the way people thought. You were
either an activist or not. Then petrol came back and order was restored. It was
just a bourgeois revolution and it failed.'

Kurys denied that *Cocktail Molotov* was actually a sequel to *Diabolo menthe* or that it was based on autobiographical fact, but acknowledged instead that '[il] permet de me rappeler et de comprendre comment j'ai été, comment on m'a faite et comment je suis aujourd'hui'[4] (Wachthausen 1980). The film unfurls as a fictional narrative, but the collective 'nous' of the afterword alerts the spectator to the director's identification with her central protagonists, if retrospectively, 'C'était presque l'été et l'essence était revenue/Et on voulait nous faire croire que tout était fini/ Pour nous le voyage venait de commencer'.[5] There are also obvious continuities with the family set-up of *Diabolo menthe*. The central character, now the elder of the two daughters, is named Anne, the sisters live in Paris with their divorced mother (who has a new partner and a more ostentatiously bourgeois life style), and the absent father is played by Michel Puterflam again. Interviews given by Kurys point to other autobiographical elements. Like the fictional Anne, Kurys fell in love when she was a teenager, ran away from home and planned to go to a kibbutz, though these events in her life took place before 1968. Similarly, the triangular situation in which Anne is the object of desire of two young men, a figure which recurs in the later films *Un homme amoureux* and *Après l'amour*, is one with which Kurys claims to be familiar (Rochu 1980).

Cocktail Molotov is set in the spring and summer of 1968. Its opening pre-credit sequence sets the scene for the generational conflict which follows. Two young men, Fred (Philippe Lebas) and Bruno (François Cluzet), enter a theatre where Anne (Elise Caron) is sitting in the audience with her mother (Geneviève Fontanel) and her stepfather; Fred jumps on to the stage with a loudhailer and proclaims that he loves Anne but that her parents have prevented her from seeing him; after the show the parents discover that their car, an expensive white Citroën DS, has been daubed with graffiti: 'Merde', 'Love' and 'Anne Je t'aime'. In the

4 'allows me to remember and to understand the way I was, how I was formed and what I am like to-day'.

5 'It was almost summer and petrol had come back/And they wanted us to believe that it was all over/For us the journey had just begun.'

car on the way home, Anne smiles to herself as the handclapping rhythm of the guitar-based soundtrack recalls May 1968 and the (unvoiced) slogan 'Ce n'est qu'un début/continuons le combat!'.[6] The narrative proper begins the following day, when Anne has a violent quarrel with her mother and leaves home. She joins Fred and Bruno, plans to go to a kibbutz, and secretly spends the night with Fred in his mother's flat. When Fred is reluctant to join her on the road, she sets off alone, eventually getting a bus south in order to get the boat to Israel from Venice. Fred and Bruno catch up with her on the road and stay with her in Venice, where they learn about the May events from the press and radio. When an attractive, female Italian anarchist who puts them up for the night runs off with Anne's belongings and Bruno's 2CV, the trio decide to hitch back to Paris to take part in the events and the remaining two-thirds of the film is concerned with their adventures on the road. Anne discovers that she is pregnant and the trio go to Lyons to get help from her father, a member of the local Jewish community. Their paths divide as Anne gets taken to Switzerland for an abortion and Fred and Bruno head for Paris. Anne subsequently plans to meet them in Paris, but Fred and Bruno go to the barricades and get picked up by the police. In the final sequence, Fred and Bruno appear at Anne's window, and the trio drive off together in her stepfather's DS. The film ends on a freeze-frame of the graffiti-sprayed car in the countryside.

Cocktail Molotov has a more desultory plot than *Diabolo menthe*. The initial impetus for the narrative is provided by Anne's defiance of her mother and love for Fred. But once circumstances have prevented her from going to the kibbutz, her return to Paris, the site of the family problems she had left behind, is less purposeful. Indeed, dramatic development throughout the film is repeatedly frustrated by circumstances over which the characters seemingly have no control, be it the theft of Anne's bag and Bruno's car, Anne's pregnancy, Fred and Bruno's arrest or, more generally, their constant dependence on others for transport or financial support. The narrative focuses instead on their living

6 'It's just the beginning/Let the struggle continue!'

from day to day, their attempts at hitching rides and finding somewhere to sleep. But the episodic road movie format means that the trio's itinerary has only an oblique relationship with the drama of events taking place in Paris and elsewhere, a drama which punctuates the narrative only through their chance encounters and their access to the press and radio. The film is more concerned with examining the subtly shifting relationships between Anne, Fred and Bruno, and their experiences of life on the road such as sleeping rough, cleaning their teeth at an outdoor fountain and hitching in the rain. Brief scenes like these, not necessarily linked by a clear chain of cause and effect, produce an elliptical, fragmented structure, which for some critics precisely captures the spirit of the time, with its emphasis on freedom and spontaneity. For the film's detractors, however, the structure lacks the coherence and rhythm of *Diabolo menthe*. Its ending is particularly problematic. The impecunious trio's second departure, this time in a stolen car, leaves Anne's relationship with her family and the financial viability of her revolt unresolved. And the final freeze-frame, taken after the car has turned into a side road, undermines the suggestion of the afterword that they are embarking on a new life and that dynamic forward movement is possible.

Kurys' decision to focus on a personal story rather than on the events of May may have been due in part to budget restrictions, but the film in general refuses to use its *mise-en-scène* for scenic display or dramatic effect. As Pierre Bouteiller puts it, not only does the film evoke 'Mai 68 comme si vous n'y étiez pas',[7] it also allows the spectator to 'ne pas voir Venise et vivre'[8] (Bouteiller 1980). May is evoked visually through brief, oblique references like the graffiti-sprayed car, the posters being put up by students in Aix-en-Provence, a wedding taking place in a strike-ridden factory, people listening to de Gaulle's radio broadcast, a lorry blockade. But the moment when Bruno and Fred set out to take part in their first demonstration is shot without ambient sound and in bleached-out colour, as though muffled by fog or taking place in a dream rather than in reality. The sequence follows an

7 'May 68 as if you were not there.'
8 'not see Venice and live'.

engaging shot of children in the *banlieue* armed with dustbin lids, leaping over barricades formed by piles of old tyres, a shot which typifies the film's tangential approach to the events of May and suggests that they can be read simply as child's play. The shot recalls Bruno's playful handling of the Molotov cocktail of the title (stolen from the Italian anarchist) which he allows simply to fizzle out by the side of the mountain road. Visual spectacle is refused, too, in the images of the Italian and French landscape, which are dominated by repetitive shots of rain, darkness, litter, mud, lonely empty roads and lonely empty spaces, like the hostels and school buildings where they sleep. The *mise-en-scène* highlights the uncomfortable, everyday realities of the journey, which the trio's youth and gaiety is not always able to alleviate.

The appeal to low-key realism rather than to visual spectacle is confirmed, too, in the choice of costume and sound. *Cocktail Molotov* does not reproduce the exuberant pleasure in youth fashions which was part of the 1960s social revolution, though it does point to the way changes in fashion marked a rebellion against the older generation and allowed a *rapprochement* between the sexes. Anne's rather boyish cropped hair, Levi jeans, white shirt and beige jacket contrast sharply with the appearance of her conventional, well-groomed bourgeois mother, while the boys' hair is appropriately long. But their clothes are dull in style and colour (except for Bruno's long red scarf), and signs of visual extravagance are to be glimpsed elsewhere, in the cameo appearance of a comic long-haired beatnik (Christian Clavier), in the wonderfully flared jeans of a lorry-driver (Patrick Chesnais), in the scene of the mini-skirted hippy wedding, glimpsed from the point of view of Anne's outraged stepfather. Similarly, the film does not reproduce the pleasure in rock music characteristic of the late 1960s except in the long shot of the trio dancing in the back of a lorry and the scene where they are hitching in the rain to the sound of a (non-diegetic) blues guitar. Rather than using authentic period music, the film uses Yves Simon's incidental music, as in *Diabolo menthe*, to create a sense of nostalgia at certain key moments: Anne leaving home, making love for the first time, watching the boats in Venice with Fred and deciding to go back to

Paris 'so as not to miss everything'; Bruno feeling excluded; the jubilant strikers; and the links between Anne and Fred in the parallel sequence near the end in which Fred grieves for his dying father and Anne writes to him from the abortion clinic. The words of Simon's songs, translated into English and sung by Murray Head (and no doubt intended to recall the California-style music of 'the summer of love'), provide a slightly patronising, sentimental commentary on each stage of Anne's trajectory – her solitary journey south, the return to Paris, and her final departure from home.

Although the narrative structure and *mise-en-scène* of *Cocktail Molotov* do not address the events of May 1968 directly, the attempt to imbricate a personal narrative into the narrative of national events is more striking than in *Diabolo menthe*. Certainly the film does not provide the spectator with any solid understanding of the history of the student uprising and the workers' protest movement which followed. Rather it scatters references to names and incidents likely to trigger memories for those already familiar with the events: the student barricades, student leaders Alain Geismar and Jacques Sauvageot, the violence of the French riot police (the CRS),[9] the strikes, de Gaulle's broadcast to the nation, the lack of petrol and vegetables. But its focus on personal revolt ties in with the social revolution underpinning May 1968 which called into question conventional hierarchies and divisions in French society. Anne's revolt against her bourgeois mother, motivated by her mother's unjustifiable refusal to let her see her working-class boyfriend, highlights the rigidities and prejudices of the bourgeoisie and their abuse of power. Her love affair with Fred signals that generational conflict is more significant than class differences, and the young people's casual encounters on the road, theoretically at least, point to the possibility of an alternative, more fluid society than that of the Fifth Republic presided over by de Gaulle.

However, the film's attitude to the father figure as representative of power and authority is actually problematic and

9 Compagnie républicaine de sécurité.

ambivalent. Certainly, by centring on the point of view of Anne, Fred and Bruno, the film is critical of paternal authority figures like Anne's father who ridicules the aspirations of the students, her stepfather, Bertrand, who opposes the strike action taking place in his factory, and Fred's working-class father who believes in the need for a 'strong man' to lead the country out of crisis. But these characters are not shown as strong, powerful figures. Anne's father is mild-mannered and weak, Bertrand has been outmanoeuvred by his workforce, Fred's father is dying. Similarly, the middle-aged male drivers they meet on the road are primarily objects of ridicule, like the pompous bourgeois who thinks the student demonstrations are merely a form of protest against 'papa' because the younger generation has not had the Resistance or the Algerian war to help it assert its identity. Nor do the elders in the Jewish Community Centre in Lyons, who are seen listening with approval to de Gaulle's speech abjuring violence, constitute a threat. A member of the CRS encountered in Aix-en-Provence, a veteran of the Algerian war, is even reduced to tears by the thought of the violence taking place on the streets of Paris and, in a monologue similar to Pascale's description of the Charonne massacre in *Diabolo menthe*, makes links between the deployment of the CRS against the students and the torture exercised by the French army in Algeria. There is no confrontation between the trio and their fathers – Fred weeps for his, Anne depends on hers for her abortion, the trio depend on Bertrand's car for their second escape – and this lack of parallel between the personal and the national narrative (epitomised by the graffito in the metro station 'papa pue')[10] is typical of the film's ambivalence towards the events of May.

Nevertheless, the film still constructs a clear-cut divide between the generations. It is the younger generation, fleetingly glimpsed through figures like the *lycée* student, striking workers and fleeing demonstrators, who are most clearly involved in alternative political action. The spontaneous, defiant behaviour of the central trio provides a marked contrast with adult conformity through acts like Fred's taking over the stage of the Odéon theatre (a

10 'daddy stinks'.

privileged site, which recalls the occupation of the Odéon during the May events) and breaking the convent rules (and washbasin) in order to make love with Anne; or Bruno sleeping with the Italian anarchist, shrugging off the theft of his car, and pretending to collect money for Jewish youth; or Fred and Bruno climbing on to Anne's balcony before setting off on the road again. However, the nature and extent of the trio's revolt is not commensurate with the political enthusiasms generated by May 1968. In fact they meet few other young people on the road, and no articulate, passionate supporter of political action. Though 'solidarity' appears in the graffiti, the journey generates little solidarity and, indeed, the activities of the only clearly-marked political character, the Italian anarchist, are confined to having sex with Bruno and then stealing his car and Anne's belongings. Similarly, the lorry driver taking flowers to Paris for Mother's Day is not concerned about not being on strike. It is also notable that the three young protagonists are generally unable or unwilling to engage in dialogue or debate in the presence of adults and so challenge the hierarchies of power. Though their tacit support of the events is unquestionable, they do not articulate any political views – as Bruno declares, 'C'est la grève, c'est la guerre, je ne sais pas ce que c'est ...'[11] – and, as has already been made clear, the exploding of the Molotov cocktail and the attempt to take part in the demonstration in Paris are peculiarly ineffective, as is Anne's desire to go to a kibbutz. The characters are involved in a quest for personal freedom rather than seeking to change the world, and the film does not represent the very real hopes for social and political change that were felt at the time.

However, the commitment to personal freedom is significant to the extent that it is focalised through the point of view of Anne, the primary subject of the narrative. Anne is portrayed as a proud, independent seventeen-year-old who is less amenable than the usual French *gamine* (epitomised in the 1980s by Charlotte Gainsbourg in films like, *L'Effrontée* (Claude Miller 1985))[12] and displays an

---

11 'It's a strike, it's war, I don't know what it is ...'

12 A more sympathetic account of the need for separation between mother and daughter can be found in Charlotte Dubreuil's *Ma chérie* (1980).

awkward mix of coldness and tenderness. Her assertion of independence is linked with her drive to separate from her mother and claim control over her body and her sexuality. On leaving home, she gets a packet of contraceptive pills from a friend (a doctor's daughter) and makes love to Fred for the first time, the camera providing discrete before and after two-shots of the protagonists, rather than inscribing a conventional male gaze. When Fred seems disinclined to leave for Israel with her, she sets out on the road alone, though the sight of a leering male driver forces her to take the bus instead of hitching on her own. When she meets up with Fred and Bruno again, she is able to enjoy a teasingly platonic friendship with Bruno as well as sustaining her relationship with Fred. It is she who makes the decision to return to Paris, and if she throws away her bra in the course of the journey, she is also aware of the power relations generated by sexual difference and insists to Bruno that rape is a real issue for women. She faces up to her unplanned pregnancy with apparent equanimity, uses her visit to the doctor to enquire why she has never experienced sexual pleasure, and takes a pragmatic approach to the necessity for an abortion, even though it means asking her father for help. Anne thus establishes her right to take the initiative, act independently and dispose of her body as she wishes without feeling guilty or inadequate.

Although *Cocktail Molotov* does map out the agenda which was to be taken up by the women's movement in the years following 1968, the way in which it raises these issues is typically fleeting and impressionistic. Despite Anne's central role in the film, identification with her is rendered difficult by the fragmented narrative structure, the use of mid-shots rather than close-ups, her difficulty in making eye contact with others, and the lack of articulation of her feelings. Her attitude to losing her virginity is taken for granted, her ignorance of how contraception works glossed over, her feelings in relation to her pregnancy and abortion minimised.[13] The film draws no conclusions from the paradoxical situation in which, abortion being illegal in France,

13 A more brutal representation of teenage female sexuality from a girl's point of view is to be found in Catherine Breillat's *36 Fillette* (1988).

she is only able to have one because her father is willing and able to finance her trip to Switzerland, and the significance of the event is minimised by an ellipsis which cuts straight to her recovery, intercut with events taking place in Paris. There are also limitations on the degree of sexual freedom which the characters claim, either for themselves or others. They may break with the moral codes relating to sex before marriage, but there is no exploration of alternative sexual relationships. Hints at intimacy between Anne and Bruno are not developed, the friendship between Bruno and Fred is muted, and homosexuality is figured only through a crazy driver who makes a grotesque pass at Fred. Anne's rites of passage, then, do not lead to a more mature understanding of or tolerance for others. And, despite her proto-feminist trajectory, her return home does not allow for a resolution of the initial mother/daughter conflict.

The relative lack of discussion about Anne's feelings may be in part a function of the fact that in this film, unlike *Diabolo menthe*, relationships between women are marginalised. Anne's little sister Sophie has only a brief appearance at the beginning of the narrative (when she offers Anne her piggy-bank savings) and at the end; a girlfriend appears only briefly to give Anne the pill; the Italian anarchist is a rival who steals her belongings; and the woman doctor cannot imagine that pregnancy might be unwelcome. Anne identifies with her boyfriends rather than her girlfriends, two attractive young men who confound normative representations of masculinity. Fred and Bruno are set decorators who, in the spirit of May 1968, temporarily abandon their jobs to follow Anne. Despite their different class backgrounds, they are both young and pretty, sensitive and romantic and marked by tragedy (the death of a woman they both loved, also called Anne). They apparently have no other purpose than to care for Anne, and to some extent each other, though they also experience jealousy of each other at various points. Bruno, who is subject to bouts of loneliness, shares references to Rimbaud with Anne, lends her clothing to keep her warm, and accompanies her to the doctor in Fred's absence, pretending to be her husband. Fred, who sheds a tear when his reactionary father lies dying in hospital, provides her with physical tenderness and, after his initial moody reaction to her pregnancy, helps her approach her father for help with securing the abortion. Despite their ability to give emotional support when on the road, however, the film highlights how ineffectual Fred and Bruno are in the wider world when they get caught after leaving the metro to attend the demonstration, just as others are desperately trying to escape from it. 'On est vraiment des cons',[14] says Bruno, a judgement which the film invites the spectator affectionately to agree with.

Cocktail Molotov's lack of euphoria and the ineffectualness of the young people it portrays can to some extent be explained by Kurys' strong authorial presence at the end of the film. The words of the song to 'Dearest Anne', 'Wish I was with you walking by your side, wish I was young again and could see life through your eyes, but ...', comment on youth from the point of view of the older, more cynical adult. The patronising 'but' introduces a 1980 perspective on May 1968 which concedes that the events failed to achieve their ideals, and undermines the significance of the characters' actions. Indeed, the behaviour of the young people can be read as more like that of disaffected young people in the late 1970s: 'Apolitiques, un brin égoistes, claquant la porte aux parents, utilisant la contraception et l'avortement comme objets de consommation courante, ils font partie de cette jeunesse – parfois désenchantée – pour qui le "principe de plaisir" et les tentatives d'escapades priment sur ce que Marcuse, guru de Mai, appelait le "principe de réalité", c'est-à-dire la confrontation avec les tensions quotidiennes'[15] (Montvalon 1980). The young protagonists of *Cocktail Molotov*, who benefit from the climate of May 1968 without themselves making a political commitment, become the objects of a distanced critical authorial gaze. Kurys' afterword may suggest some hope for the future ('the journey had

14 'We're really stupid!'
15 'Apolitical and rather selfish, slamming the door on their parents, using contraception and abortion like everyday consumer goods, they belong to those often disillusioned young people for whom the 'pleasure principle' and attempts to escape are more important than what Marcuse, the guru of May, called the 'reality principle', i.e. the confrontation with the tensions of everyday life.'

just begun'), but the film's narrative, sound and image work to deny the credibility of such a position.

Cocktail Molotov's ambivalent take on May 1968 is also determined by the fact that the film is used to explore problematic relationships within the family, particularly between the daughter and her mother and father. Kurys has described her representation of the father as typical of 'mon image du père, absent, occasionnel'.[16] The relationship between father and daughter at first appears to be affectionate and easy, even though they have not seen each other for a long time. Certainly the father, who is recognisably Jewish (he speaks Yiddish to his shop assistant), understands Anne's predicament and is willing to help her sort it out. But as the situation progresses it becomes clear that, though he is unassuming and unimpressive, he still wants to give Anne unwelcome advice on what to do, like stopping smoking, and his idea of buying an electric razor in Switzerland where it is cheaper falls in with a perceived stereotypical preoccupation with money. Nevertheless, his relationship with Anne contrasts favourably with the antagonistic relationship between Anne and her mother, who is the real focus for anger and revolt in this film. Glamorous but unsympathetic, snobbish and authoritarian, the mother demonstrates the hypocrisy, snobbery and arrogance of her class in her refusal to accept Anne's sexuality and let her see Fred. The fight between mother and daughter, sparked off by the mother's anger at the vandalisation of Bertrand's car and Anne's scornful rejection of her mother's point of view, constitutes the most brutal scene of the film. Shot with a moving camera which produces flurried images and edited with quick cuts, their violent verbal and then physical clash is extremely shocking. The mother hits her daughter with unacceptable force and the daughter responds in kind, accusing her mother of hating her and being jealous of her, until she is beaten to the floor. The scene is witnessed by the little sister who tries desperately to intervene. The entire film is thus based on Anne's antagonism towards the mother, a woman who initially represents power and authority but who is turned at the

16 'my image of the father, someone who is absent, only around from time to time'.

end into an object of mockery, a woman who has been ill with measles. The relentlessly negative representation of the mother is consonant with the experiences of many feminists in the 1970s who blamed their mothers for initiating them into the values of a patriarchal society.[17] But in *Cocktail Molotov* it also derives from the daughter's feelings of exclusion in the context of the fragmented nuclear family.

The film contains an emblematic shot which expresses Anne's solitude and isolation. In the course of her visit to her father, she finds herself in the room she must have occupied prior to her parents' divorce. In semi-darkness, the camera zooms in on the mirror and then pans around the room, taking in traces of her former childhood possessions alongside the slabs of fabric belonging to her father. The scene ends on Anne, awaiting the outcome of Fred's talk with her father, moving to stare out of the window, alone and silent. If Anne's journey in *Cocktail Molotov* can be read as an attempt to move beyond the unsatisfactory relationships she has had with her parents, and establish a new set of interpersonal relations based on her autonomy, her continuing anger towards her mother and dependency on her father (and stepfather) suggest that that attempt has been only partially successful.

Cocktail Molotov's particular representation of female experiences at the time of May 1968 may not have appealed to contemporary audiences in 1980 but the film still makes an important contribution to a predominantly male-centred French cinema. May 1968 to date has rarely been directly addressed in French cinema, though its influence underpinned filmic output throughout the 1970s. Films which make reference to May 1968 prior to *Cocktail Molotov* have been characterised by Michel Perez as either 'naively idealistic or heavily doctrinaire'[18] (Perez 1980) and, as Keith Reader (1993) points out, Louis Malle's later *Milou*

17 Feminist fiction of the 1970s is often critical of the mother, for example Marie Cardinal's shocking representation of her mother as drunk and incontinent in *Les Mots pour le dire* (1976).

18 For example, *Les Indiens sont encore loin* (Patricia Moraz 1977), *La Carapate* (Gérard Oury 1978), *Courage fuyons* (Yves Robert 1979).

en mai (1989) is as oblique as Kurys' film and lacks any footage of the events whatsoever. Kurys' focus on day-to-day life in May from the point of view of teenagers who actually miss out on the events is an interesting attempt to examine the impact of the historical moment on ordinary lives, even if in the process the film misses the opportunity of reinscribing the presence of girls and women into the political debates and historical events of the period. But *Cocktail Molotov* also serves another function, namely a reworking of the male-dominated genre of the road movie. Kurys wanted to produce a riposte to *Les Valseuses* (Bertrand Blier 1974), a film whose misogynist treatment of women by its two central protagonists (played by Gérard Depardieu and Patrick Dewaere) gave offence to many spectators. However, while *Cocktail Molotov*'s male characters offer a positive alternative to the grotesque machismo of Blier's heroes, Elise Caron's Anne lacks Miou-Miou's charisma and is unable to carry a film whose narrative structure and *mise-en-scène* are already problematic.

As with *Diabolo menthe*, *Cocktail Molotov*'s study of adolescence can be seen to be giving a female-centred inflection to the subject matter of Truffaut's films. The opening scene at the Odéon is reminiscent of the opening scene at the Salle Pléyel in *L'Amour à vingt ans* (1962) where Antoine Doinel points out Colette, the object of his desire, to his friend René, with the important difference that in *Cocktail Molotov* it is the female protagonist who becomes the subject of the narrative. *Cocktail Molotov* can also be compared to *Jules et Jim* (1961) as a film in which two friends are in love with the same woman; but, again, Kurys privileges the female over the male point of view and refuses Truffaut's tragic ending and the fetishised, idealised image of woman embodied in Jeanne Moreau's Catherine. Kurys also includes the Jewish community in her representation of French society, and the scene in *Cocktail Molotov* where the elders of the Jewish Community Centre in Lyons listen approvingly to de Gaulle's speech to the nation suggests a humorous reworking of the scene in *La Fille du puisatier* (Marcel Pagnol 1940) where the villagers of Occupied France listen to Maréchal Pétain. However, if *Cocktail Molotov* is compared with other French women's films of the late 1970s, it lacks the originality of Coline Serreau's exploration of a triangular relationship in *Pourquoi pas!* (1977) and rather prematurely takes abortion for granted, instead of raising it as an issue, as in the feminist documentary, *Histoires d'A* (Marielle Issartel and Charles Belmont 1973) and Agnès Varda's *L'Une chante l'autre pas* (1977).

Though Kurys has claimed that the film identifies the elements of social change which were to mark the 1970s, 'Tout y est en germe, le féminisme, l'écologie, l'évolution du langage, des mœurs ...' (Rouchy 1980),[19] *Cocktail Molotov* is rendered problematic by Kurys' distancing of herself from the events and through its focus on a personal trajectory which, apart from its claiming of women's rights over their bodies and their sexuality, runs counter to the narrative of political action suggested by the film's title. Indeed, the characters' absence from the events of May can perhaps be read as a dramatisation of Kurys' characters' more general feelings of exclusion. The sense that the characters are onlookers rather than participants in life may account in part for the film's failure to create empathy with its characters, as may its inability to embrace fully the subjectivity of its central female character.

References

Bouteiller, Pierre (1980), 'Mai 68 en creux', *Quotidien de Paris*, 12 February.
Lejeune, Paule (1987), *Le Cinéma des femmes: 105 femmes cinéastes d'expression française (France, Belgique, Suisse) 1895–1987*, Paris, Editions Atlas Lherminier.
Montvalon, Christine de (1980), '*Cocktail Molotov* loin des barricades', *Télérama*, 6 February.
Perez, Michel (1980), '*Cocktail Molotov* de Diane Kurys, Grenadine lacrymogène', *Le Matin*, 2 February.
Reader, Keith with Wadia, Khurscheed (1993), *The May 1968 Events in France*, New York, St Martin's Press, 140–7.
Rochu, Gilbert (1980), 'Mémoire d'une jeune fille publique', *Libération*, 6 February.
Rouchy, Marie-Elisabeth (1980), '*Cocktail Molotov* au cocktail menthe', *Le Matin*, 6 February.
Wachthausen, Jean-Luc (1980), 'Mai 68 en stop pour trois adolescents', *Le Figaro*, 5 February.

19 'Everything is there in embryonic form: feminism, ecology, change in language, change in lifestyle ...'

3

Coup de foudre

In the course of a series of interviews with her mother, intended as the basis for a film about her own childhood, Kurys became fascinated instead by her mother's past. In her third film, *Coup de foudre*, she documents the extraordinary circumstances in which her mother, Léna, met Michel, her husband, then a decade later Madeleine, her friend, and subsequently left her husband at the age of thirty-two, with two small children, to lead an independent life in Paris. The women's friendship lasted over twenty-five years, but Madeleine died two years before the film was made and Kurys' mother died just before the film opened. At the time of the interviews, Kurys was the same age as her mother had been when her marriage broke up, but the unmarried, childless Kurys did not personally identify with her mother's story, declaring in interviews that she found her mother's 'passionate friendship' hard to understand (Manceaux 1983) and that it had been a source of her suffering as a child, 'Ça a eu des résonances, ça a fait mal à des êtres ...'[1] (Tranchant 1983). For her, the film was not just a tribute to her mother, whom she acknowledged as a source of her own strength and independence, but also a way of confronting her traumatic childhood, expiating the guilt she felt about her parents' separation, and retrieving something of what had been lost. 'J'ai ressenti longtemps un sentiment de culpabilité. J'ai cru qu'ils se séparaient à cause de moi. Avec ce film je

1 'It had repercussions, it hurt people ...'

me suis libérée'² (Fournier 1983). In fact *Coup de foudre* is dedicated to all three of the main participants in the drama and its title applies as much to Michel's falling for Léna as for the relationship between Léna and Madeleine. Though *Coup de foudre* centres on the mother's story, its detailed reconstruction of two key periods in her mother's life produces a complex, multi-layered portrait which interweaves Kurys' admiration for her mother's drive for independence with her distress for the abandoned father and the vulnerable child.

Before proceeding to analyse the film, it is worth noting how the mother–daughter relationship is frequently ignored, obscured or mystified in dominant cinema. As Adrienne Rich once famously argued, the 'cathexis between mother and daughter – essential, distorted, misused – is the great unwritten story' (Walters 1992: 3). Conventional discourses on motherhood depend on 'the old angel/witch dichotomy' (Kaplan 1992: 183) and blame the daughter's neuroses on either the too loving mother's self-sacrificing overinvestment in her, or on her unloving absence and neglect. The double bind of mothering is compounded by the supposition that the daughter can only achieve adult femininity within a patriarchal society by separating from the mother, even though, paradoxically, femininity is also associated with the reproduction of mothering. Arguably, early feminist scholarship initially accepted concepts and paradigms destructive to the possibility of mother–daughter intimacy and continuity, blaming the mother for the daughter's incorporation into patriarchal ideology. Only at a later stage in feminist theory has the power and creativity of mothers been valorised (Fischer 1996: 10). Yet the mother–daughter relationship is central to women's individual development (Fischer 1996: 198), and central to a feminist project of recognising shared womanhood. Both Walters and Fischer point to the need for representations which refuse what Walters refers to as 'tedious tales of maternal martyrdom and malice' (Walters 1992: 229). According to Fischer, such representations are to be found 'in the genre of feminist "matrilinear" [documentary]

2 'For a long time I felt guilty. I thought they were separating because of me. This film enabled me to liberate myself.'

cinema, [where] we find daughters celebrating and speaking for their mothers, removing them from the realm of essentialism and locating them within the frames of race and history' (Fischer 1996: 30). In *Coup de foudre*, the author–director–daughter turns away from the tale of maternal malice reproduced in *Cocktail Molotov* and instead speaks for her mother, 'Sa parole s'est arrêtée, et maintenant c'est moi qui dois la transmettre à quelqu'un d'autre'[3] (Fournier 1983). The result is a complex work which is open to multiple readings, as a 'woman's film', a lesbian film, a heritage film and a work of auto/biography.

After writing the first draft of the screenplay on her own, Kurys spent a year reworking it with her friend Alain Le Henry. *Coup de foudre* was the first of Kurys' films to enjoy a relatively large budget (16,000,000 francs) and the first to be shot in Cinemascope, with star actors Isabelle Huppert, Miou-Miou and Guy Marchand in the lead roles, alongside the lesser known Jean-Pierre Bacri. It opened to huge publicity, with a red-carpet gala evening at *Chez Maxim's*, including a display of period cars. The film subsequently became one of the ten most popular films of 1983 in France and won the 1984 Prix de l'Académie nationale du cinéma. It gave rise to a novel, authored by Olivier Cohen and Kurys (1983), based on the screenplay. It was also extremely successful in the United States and received an Oscar nomination for best foreign-language film. It provided a European gloss on the themes of women's independence and female friendship to be found in American films like *An Unmarried Woman* (Paul Mazursky 1977), *Girlfriends* (Claudia Weill 1977), *The Turning Point* (Herbert Ross 1977), *Julia* (Fred Zinnemann 1977) and *Lianna* (John Sayles 1983). Yet by 1983, the representation of a proto-feminist revolt against an unsatisfactory marriage in the 1950s was not in itself particularly controversial.[4] Indeed, in the years following the election of François Mitterrand and the Socialist Party in 1981, many in France thought that feminism had already achieved its goals (Duchen 1986: 125–49;

3 'Her voice has ceased and now it's up to me to transmit her words to others.'
4 Aline Issermann's *Le Destin de Juliette* (1983) is another study of an unhappy marriage set in the past, this time in a rural setting, seen from the point of view of the submissive but resentful wronged wife.

Holmes 1996: 213–15). Even if *Coup de foudre*'s narrative of female consciousness-raising and its privileging of women-centred relationships give it a special place within dominant French cinema of the early 1980s, its success may be attributable to the pleasures of its star performances and its retro *mise-en-scène* as much as to its thematic preoccupations.

At the time of the making of *Coup de foudre*, French cinema had already started to turn to what has now been styled 'heritage' cinema,[5] even if, as Michel Perez notes, the 1950s were still virtually virgin territory for retro filmmaking:

> L'époque, elle a ceci de privilégié que le laminoir de la mode rétro ne l'a pas encore réellement réduite à l'état d'objet de consommation, de mythe manufacturé. Il n'y a pas encore, au cinéma, de code de représentation des années cinquante: c'est un terrain à peu près vierge où il est passionnant de chercher les racines de ce qui prolifère aujourd'hui, les roses et les épines[6] (Perez 1983).

Kurys invested tremendous energy in establishing the authenticity of the look and sounds of *Coup de foudre*, formalising her attachment to the film's *mise-en-scène* for the production of a sense of the 'real',

> Un film est un plein sac de détails qui le rendent crédible. Le réalisateur est placé constamment devant un choix, il doit décider à chaque instant: de l'intonation d'une voix, du nombre de passants, de la couleur d'une voiture ... cette force devait servir un film vrai, tendre et cruel à la fois, comme la vie[7] (Cornuz-Langlois 1983).

She exercised personal control over all the details of the *mise-en-*

---

5 For a general discussion of heritage cinema, see Andrew Higson (1993). For specific discussion of French heritage cinema, see Guy Austin (1996), and Ginette Vincendeau (1995).

6 'The period is privileged in that the retro fashion bulldozer has not yet reduced it to a consumer object, a manufactured myth: it's an almost virgin territory in which it's fascinating to look for the roots of the roses and thorns of today.'

7 'A film is a bundle of details which make it credible. The filmmaker is constantly confronted with a choice, he [*sic*] has to make a decision about the intonation of a voice, the number of passers-by, the colour of a car ... this power must lead to a film which is true, tender and cruel at the same time, like life.'

scène, from the suitcases and shoes worn by the three thousand extras to the shape of the period refrigerator. Huppert and Miou-Miou even wore 1950s perfume on set because she wanted to jog memories of smells, like the scent of rice powder and Soir de Paris in her mother's handbags. She tracked down rare recordings of popular jingles and radio programmes for the soundtrack and incorporated Glen Miller's big-band music, and Perry Como singing (ironically) 'I wonder who's kissing her now' as a framing song to the narrative of Léna and Michel's marital breakdown. The question is whether the surface pleasures of sound and image displace attention from the issues raised by the narrative or serve rather to locate the characters within a precise historical framework. Does the film provide 'a sociological document, a minutely observed cameo about French middle-class life – and the sexual and social revolution that eroded its very foundations' (Behr 1983) or does it get bogged down in period detail, 'Le beau parcours de femmes se perd dans une nostalgie rétro-racoleuse ... L'arrière-plan 'socio-politico-culturel' ambitieusement suggéré par la réalisatrice, semble artificiel'[8] (Pascaud 1983)? Alternatively, is the plenitude of the *mise-en-scène* a way of compensating for the absence and loss represented by the narrative?

Coup de foudre is set first in the war years, 1942–44, then in Lyons from 1952–54. The narrative is structured by the development of the relationship between Léna (Isabelle Huppert) and Madeleine (Miou-Miou), and builds up to a dramatic climax which has serious and irreversible repercussions on the lives of all the main characters, including Sophie (Saga Blanchard), the younger daughter, who witnesses the final moment of separation between Léna and her husband Michel (Guy Marchand). The link between the two women is first established through a long prologue set during the Occupation and Liberation of France, which predates their meeting but suggests why and how they come to mean so much to each other. This opening sequence crosscuts through parallel editing between the story of Léna, a young Jewish woman

8 'The beautiful trajectory of the women gets lost in eye-catching retro nostalgia ... The "socio-politico-cultural" background, ambitiously suggested by the filmmaker, seems artificial.'

who escapes from a French deportation camp by agreeing to marry Michel, a French legionnaire (who also turns out to be Jewish), in whose company she then escapes from Occupied France, and the story of Madeleine, a newly married Bohemian art student whose husband is shot dead by the Milice. Music and editing link the two women survivors and invite the spectator to be moved by their experiences, one the victim of French anti-Semitism, the other of French Fascism. The moment of their meeting is produced through a trick of the editing which fuses the balloon-filled sky over the Liberation celebrations in Lyons with the sky over a school in 1952 where a Christmas concert is being held, as though no event inbetween (including the birth of their children) is of any comparable significance. The intensity of their attraction for one another can be understood through the juxtaposition of the traumas of their wartime experiences and the dullness of their provincial, married lives.

The plot of *Coup de foudre* proceeds through short, succinct scenes which are not linked as tightly as in classic narrative but succeed one another affectively or chronologically. The feelings and emotions experienced by the women and their husbands are developed in a subtle fashion, as in a musical quartet, with small incidents marking shifts in the relationships. Cutaway shots of the children introduce an alternative, muted perspective on events. After the (understated) *coup de foudre* of Léna's meeting with Madeleine, the two women become virtually inseparable. An extended montage sequence depicts them getting to know one another. When Léna eventually introduces Madeleine and her husband Costa (Jean-Pierre Bacri) to Michel, Madeleine mischievously suggests that perhaps Léna and Michel are not suited as a couple. Léna becomes aware of the frustrations of her life as Michel's wife, Madeleine becomes less able to deal with Costa's inadequacies, and Michel starts to become jealous of Madeleine. A brief montage sequence shows the women starting to look for work, then planning to set up a boutique together in Lyons. However, Madeleine leaves Costa and moves to Paris, thinking Léna will join her. Léna spends a weekend in Paris, having told Michel she is visiting her mother's grave in Antwerp, but feels unable to leave Michel so abruptly and returns to Lyons to face Michel's anger at her deception. Michel forbids her to see Madeleine again and a period of separation follows, represented by a montage sequence in which voice-over readings of their correspondence dominate the soundtrack while the image track, after a view of Paris, presumably from Madeleine's point of view, shows Léna first letting the milk boil over while she reads, then setting up a boutique in Lyons on her own. When her last letters are returned unopened, Léna discovers from Costa that Madeleine has had a breakdown. She rescues Madeleine from her parents' house, takes her back to the boutique, Magdalena, on its opening day, and tells her it's the happiest day of her life. Just as they are celebrating their reunion, Michel arrives with a potted plant, sees Madeleine and goes berserk, destroying the boutique. Léna then leaves Michel and, when he arrives at the villa by the seaside in Normandy where she is staying with Madeleine, she asks him to leave. The film ends with a series of shots of the participants in this familial drama, all in separate frames or separate spaces within the frame, the plenitude of a happy ending denied.

Its problematic ending aside, *Coup de foudre* is structured like a romance in which two people overcome the obstacles in the way of the formation of their couple, in this case, unusually, not a hetero-sexual couple (the women are not interested in either their own or each other's husband, despite the men's advances), but a relation-ship between women, lending credence to the way the film has been read as a lesbian art movie (Merck 1986). The narrative is also a feminist consciousness-raising exercise to the extent that it invites the spectator to share in Léna and Madeleine's growing awareness of their unsatisfactory lives as married women in the pre-feminist patriarchal world of the 1950s. However, the film's ending introduces another perspective through its afterword, 'Mon père est parti au petit jour/Il n'a plus jamais revu ma mère/Madeleine est morte maintenant il y a deux ans'.[9] As Jean Rochereau puts it, these three horrifying sentences give the film its measure as

9 'My father left at dawn/He never saw my mother again/It is now two years since Madeleine died.'

'une blessure inguérissable'[10] (Rochereau 1983). This afterword, which provoked both tears and applause on the part of contemporary spectators, reveals that what had appeared to be fictional is actually autobiographical, and that the little girl whose longing gaze structures the final image represents Diane Kurys herself as a child. As Catherine Portuges notes, 'This auto-biographical appendix necessitates an immediate retrospective revision by the spectator, who thus becomes a more than usually active participant in the autobiographical process' (Portuges 1988: 345). Although the film's narrative structure authenticates Léna and Madeleine's struggle for self-determination, the child's gaze and the adult daughter's authorial postscript (which, literally, puts the father first), undermine any simplistic pleasure in the outcome of that struggle. The viewer is invited to reflect retro-spectively on the daughter's suffering, caused not just by the loss of the father but also by the impact of the mother's relationship with Madeleine. At the end, Sophie is repositioned at the centre of the frame as the object of her mother's concerned look, as she had been in the early sequence of the school concert, before Léna met Madeleine, while she in turn looks longingly at the father she is about to lose. The complexity of the composition of these final images, which fix Sophie's loss, Léna and Michel's separation, and the fragmentation of the alternative family formed by Léna, Madeleine and their children, is indicative of the complex set of narratives and identifications which the film weaves together, and its refusal to sacrifice the messiness of realistically represented interpersonal relationships in favour of an uncritical endorsement of the mother's position.

The film's period reconstruction is not used gratuitously but artfully expresses the constraints within which the characters live out their lives, from the crowd and action scenes of the wartime sequences to the more intimate and enclosed public and domestic spaces of the 1950s. The film incorporates point-of-view shots which prevent the image track from being appropriated just by the pleasures of nostalgic looking. The opening establishing shot of

10 'an incurable wound'.

mountain scenery and period bus arriving in the distance, cuts immediately to a shot of Huppert as Léna sitting at the back of the bus full of women, then to shots of the landscape and the arrival at Rivesaltes from Léna's point of view. The spectator's perspective on events, including Léna's friendship with a woman prisoner and her meeting with Michel, is thus determined by identification with Léna. Similarly, in the 1950s scenes, panning shots of domestic interiors crammed with period artefacts are focalised through the characters, as when Madeleine's art-filled studio/ living-room is represented through Léna's fascinated, lingering gaze; or when Léna's apartment is first seen as the camera follows Michel's return home from work. Place and space also function to establish the women's need for autonomy. Madeleine's creativity is stifled in her parents' oppressive, bourgeois house and in the flat she shares with the bungling Costa. Léna's flat is the site of Michel's jealousy and aggression, provoked by signs of Madeleine's influence, like her gift of a potted Japanese garden or her loan of a sexy, black dress. Forced out of the home, because domestic interiors are sites of conflict, the women provisionally take over other spaces, like the park, the cloakroom at the swimming baths, Léna's car and, especially, Léna's fashion boutique, or leave Lyons altogether, as in the trip to Paris and at the end, the escape to Cabourg. However, the spaces the women create are always under threat of disruption, and the narrative climaxes with Michel's paroxysm of violence and the destruction of the boutique, witnessed by other women peering in through the window.

Coup de foudre's use of 1950s fashions may provide nostalgic viewing pleasures but it also gives meaning to the progression of the women's friendship. The way the women look (and smell) is part of their attraction for each other as well as being a key element of the narrative. When they first meet, the difference in their appearance is notable. Bourgeois Léna, in blue suit, hat with veil, and fur coat, is shocked and fascinated by Bohemian Madeleine, in shirt and trousers, who is not wearing stockings and who offers her a smell of the sun lotion she is using on her legs. Halfway through the film, when they are searching for premises for their boutique, their outfits are virtually identical (matching long pencil skirts and high heels). When they meet again at the end, their roles have reversed. Madeleine is wearing the full-skirted flowery dress Léna had helped her sew at the beginning of their friendship, and Léna is wearing the (newly fashionable, tapered) trousers. Inbetween, their shared love of fashion and dressmaking cements their friendship, planning a boutique enables them to dream of independence, and attendance at the Balmain fashion show allows them a clandestine weekend in Paris. Fashion is a legitimate outlet for women's creativity and a refuge from the masculine world of Michel's garage and Costa's hopeless business deals. Michel's violence can thus be understood as a reaction to the fear of emasculation by and exclusion from an autonomous woman-centred world, as indicated by the blood on the hands covering his genitals (Powrie 1988: 70).

In addition to the reproduction of period settings, music and costume, the film uses Luis Bacalov's expressive incidental music to emphasise key moments of pain and suffering. Bacalov's haunting non-diegetic music, with its 'evasive strings wrapped in arabesques around the rumblings of a piano' (Hughes 1983), benefits from a distinctly Jewish inflection which provides a recurring, poignant reminder of the occasion of Léna and Michel's first meeting. It highlights key moments in the narrative: Léna's arrival in the camp, the discovery that her new husband is also Jewish, Madeleine's return home after the death of her husband, Michel's rescuing of Léna; then, the meeting of the two women, the story of Madeleine's past, Léna's doubts about her marriage, Michel playing with the girls, Léna reading to Madeleine, the two women making plans for getting a boutique, Madeleine leaving Costa; then, the separation of the couples: Michel returning by car from the Jewish cemetery in Antwerp while Léna returns from Paris in the train, Madeleine in Paris while Léna sets up her boutique in Lyons; and finally, Léna's reunion with Madeleine and Michel's discovery of his empty flat, his wife and children gone. The pathos of the music works with the retro *mise-en-scène* to invest the past with a sense of nostalgia, underlining the sense of loss which is already generated by the period setting.

However, *Coup de foudre*'s reconstruction of the 1940s and

1950s does not simply produce nostalgia for a lost golden age. Rather it invokes periods of conflict, and invests them with meanings that are grounded not just in the particular history of a secular Jewish family, but also in the more general history of wartime and postwar France. As well as reconstructing the Rivesaltes deportation camp and the activities of the Fascist Milice, its evocation of the Occupation shows women making choices and living their lives (relatively) independently, Léna by crossing into France alone, Madeleine by defying bourgeois morality and making love before her wedding. In this, it significantly pre-dates other women-centred *rétro* films like *Blanche et Marie* (Jacques Renard 1985), *Une affaire de femmes* (Claude Chabrol 1988) or *Lucie Aubrac* (Claude Berri 1997). Jewish names haunt the narrative, from the comical discovery that Lena's new husband is called Mordecaï Isaac Simon Korski (later Michel) to mention of the Steiners and the Mandels fleeing from Lyons to the gravestone in the Jewish cemetery in Antwerp which gives Léna's mother's name as Nadia Weber, née Friedman. Nevertheless, the characters' Jewishness is not made an issue in the postwar section of the film, any more than Costa's origins (his surname is Segara) or Maria the maid's, leaving spectators to make of these nominal references what they will. Nor is there more than an oblique reference to France's postwar political and military situation, figured through the presence of soldiers on leave in Léna's railway carriage.[11]

What *Coup de foudre* does do, however, is provide a critical purchase on the tensions within the family produced by France's postwar recovery and development as a consumer society. Whereas Michel, who once made money on the black market, is able to build up a successful small business and provide his family with consumer durables, like a huge fridge, a vacuum cleaner, and a small car for Léna, Léna (like other middle-class women of the time, despite getting the vote for the first time in 1944) finds herself relegated to the domestic sphere. *Coup de foudre* derives its

11 See Kristin Ross (1995), for an analysis of how the crisis in French national identity provoked by its recent history (1940–44) and its impending loss of empire was displaced onto an obsession with 'fast cars, clean bodies'.

strength from the fact that it is 'situé à une époque où rien n'était moins évident pour une femme que de décider de quitter son foyer pour vivre sa vie personnelle'[12] (Tranchant 1983). Given that, as Claire Duchen has argued, 'Women are remarkably absent from historical accounts of the Fourth Republic (1946–58) and even from accounts of the early years of the Fifth ...' (Duchen 1994: 1), *Coup de foudre* is unusual in opening up postwar social history to gendered readings. The women's sharing of their experiences reveals the limitations of their lives as wives and mothers trapped and isolated in a provincial town. Madeleine needs an outlet for her frustrated sexuality and creativity, while Léna's trajectory highlights the importance of economic, social and cultural equality within a relationship. She suffers from having no income and no chequebook of her own, and having to ask her husband's permission to learn to drive or get a job. She also discovers that she and Michel are socially and culturally mismatched. Michel has no education and no interests outside his work and his family, has difficulty communicating, and is unable to understand her need for freedom. Furthermore, he does not satisfy her sexually, as she realises when she first experiences orgasm through clandestine, non-penetrative sex with an unknown soldier (a cameo appearance by François Cluzet). Léna's and Madeleine's decision to leave their husbands and set up a new life together was unusual, revolutionary even, for 1954. The film's critique of marriage as an institution recalls the arguments of Simone de Beauvoir's *Le Deuxième sexe* (1948), but its validation of women's need for freedom and autonomy is clearly also informed by a post 1968 feminist awareness.

If the film is critical of marriage, it is not necessarily critical of men, nor of heterosexuality. Madeleine has a passionate love for and fulfilling sexual relationship with her artist husband and it is only her marriage of convenience to Costa which comes under fire, a marriage contracted in the aftermath of the Liberation when she found she was pregnant. Similarly, Léna's marriage to Michel is based on expediency and gratitude for saving her life. The

12 'situated during a period when nothing was less obvious for a woman than deciding to leave home to live her own life'.

possibility of love with a man is not completely closed over, though their encounters with other men – Carlier, the art lecturer, or the soldier on the train – are less intense than their relationship with each other. However, Costa and Michel are not represented as objects of desire. Costa is a charmingly irresponsible man who leaves his son, René, in Léna's care, so allowing her to meet Madeleine, and subsequently demonstrates his inadequacy through a series of business deals which go horribly wrong. The male dog he has bought (called Tito because it never obeys orders) has puppies, a Modigliani painting turns out to be stolen, a trainload of American shirts have only one sleeve! However, he does at least understand and accept Madeleine's behaviour and, having broken down during his hilarious mime act in a local nightclub, his last appearance in a professional stage production suggests that he too may have benefited from the break-up of his unsatisfactory marriage. In contrast, Michel's unquestioning assumption of his patriarchal role, his inability to understand his wife's needs and his progressively more pronounced violence make his position irredeemable. Yet, as Barbara Quart argues, the self-consciously balding Michel is also 'a strikingly sympathetic character' (Quart 1984: 46). Though he is not very bright, he is a hard worker, a devoted husband, and an affectionate, loving father who enjoys horsing around with the children and is devastated by the prospect of losing them. The film demonstrates that men, too, are victims of the sex/gender/class divide.

If the film is sympathetic towards men, it is nevertheless the relationship between women which is foregrounded and invested with emotion. For Pauline Kael (1984), it is a film about two women 'not having a lesbian affair', and certainly the film refuses to make their relationship sexually explicit (though Michel calls them 'des gouines').[13] Indeed, on one level they remain very formal, continuing to address each other as 'vous' not 'tu'. However, complicity between the women is the site of specific 'feminine' viewing pleasures, whether it be in scenes depicting their common tastes and interests (like reading Colette or

13 'dykes'.

swimming and dancing), or through talking about their pasts, their men and their aspirations for the future, or through momentary hints of intense desire, half-voiced but not acted upon, as when Madeleine says, 'Pourquoi je me sens si bien avec vous?'[14] or Léna confesses, 'J'ai envie de vous embrasser.'[15] The film depicts a progressive physical intimacy between the women as they exchange looks, touches, clothes and eventually hugs. They have their arms round each other when they first locate the boutique and when they celebrate their reunion. And Madeleine's breakdown when she is separated from Léna recalls the break-down she suffered after her husband's death. The absence of an authoritative male gaze and the use of two-shots, long takes and pregnant silences in scenes between the two women, strategies which are analysed in detail by Chris Straayer (1990) and Christine Holmlund (1991), enable the film to be read as the expression of lesbian desire. Whether or not the women enjoyed a sexual relationship (Kurys did not want to limit the film's audiences by making an explicitly sexual lesbian love story, but also insists that they did not), there is no gainsaying that the film invites identification with or, at least, sympathy for women who consciously put their relationship with each other before their relationships with others, and who derive their most intense pleasures from each other's company. Whilst the period setting and the women's ostensible heterosexuality mean that their relationship is less unsettling than an overtly lesbian love story would have been, there is no doubt that such a strong representation of female friendship is extremely rare in French cinema.

However, the affirmation of women's independence and friendship between women, arguably the positive elements of the mother's legacy to her daughter, is repeatedly problematised by the film's representation of the women as mothers, highlighted by cutaway shots of the children's often critical point of view on events and by the sympathetic representation of the abandoned, loving father. At the Christmas concert where Léna and Madeleine meet, where Sophie, dressed as an apple with a Maurice Chevalier

14 'Why do I feel so good when I'm with you?'
15 'I want to kiss you.'

mask, performs 'Ma Pomme' in front of her mother's loving gaze, René refuses to put on the massive Indian headdress made for him by the absent Madeleine. From the beginning, Madeleine is represented as a neglectful mother and René as a shy, disturbed child, who gets car-sick and accidentally locks himself in the toilet. The scenes of family life with Léna's more robust, rowdy daughters are most often associated with Michel's presence. Michel plays football with them at a family picnic, romps on the bed with them, sings with them in the car and at the end goes swimming with them, while Léna finds Michel's physical antics trying and prefers to spend her time with Madeleine. In fact, Léna becomes progressively less attentive as a mother, a key moment being the discovery that she and Madeleine have got on a bus without little Sophie. Sophie is eventually brought home by a furious Michel, and the film cuts from recriminations between the parents to shots of the girls framed in the doorway of their bedroom, watching Maria, the maid, and her boyfriend kissing. When the parents later quarrel over Léna's weekend in Paris, a cutaway shot shows the sobbing girls being cuddled by Maria. These inserts undermine sympathy for Léna's unhappiness and question her justification for abandoning her marriage when her children's happiness is at stake. Pain and hopelessness at the break-up of the family are underlined by Michel's discovery of the empty flat, just a family portrait left hanging on the wall, and confirmed in the final sequence, in which his tears and his sobbing voice express the loss shared by the daughter. Though Kurys may respect and admire her mother's transgressive behaviour, she also identifies with the suffering of the abandoned father.

Coup de foudre breaks with 'tales of martyrdom and malice' by reclaiming the agency and vision of a relatively ordinary woman, who is nevertheless 'an active participant in the socio-historic universe' (Fischer 1996: 210). The mother is allowed to be a complex, individuated, autonomous, sexual, adult human being. But if the film respects and validates the choices she makes, it also grieves at the lack of a more fully present, loving mother. Though Kurys claims in life to have found making the film a liberating experience, the cinematic reconstruction of her childhood does not lead to reconciliation and empowerment, but to a memorable image of the daughter's powerlessness, which she was to recreate seven years later in *La Baule Les Pins*. In the end, then, *Coup de foudre*'s representation of the mother is ambivalent. The potentially feminist narratives of women's struggle for independence and of the intense pleasures of female friendship are challenged by the final image of the lonely, vulnerable child, who, as the adult filmmaker, inherits her mother's determination to go her own way, but whose later representations of her own relationships with women are quite problematic.

References

Austin, Guy (1996), *Contemporary French Cinema: An Introduction*, Manchester and New York, Manchester University Press, 142–70.

Behr, Edward (1983), 'A Cameo of a Revolution', *Newsweek*, 9 May.

Cornuz-Langlois, Nicole (1983), 'Diane Kurys: "Ce sont les détails qui font un film", *Le Matin*, 9 April.

Duchen, Claire (1986), *Feminism in France: From May '68 to Mitterrand*, London, Boston and Henley, Routledge and Kegan Paul.

Duchen, Claire (1994), *Women's Rights and Women's Lives in France 1944–1968*, London, Routledge.

Fischer, Lucy (1996), *Cinematernity: Film, Motherhood, Genre*, Princeton, New Jersey, Princeton University Press.

Fournier, Thérèse (1983), 'Diane Kurys: en amitié, le coup de foudre est aussi fort qu'en amour', *Le Nouveau F.*, 14 April, 15.

Higson, Andrew (1993), 'Re-presenting the national past: nostalgia and pastiche in the heritage film', in Lester Friedman (ed.), *British Cinema and Thatcherism: Fires Were Started*, London, UCL Press, 109–29.

Holmes, Diana (1996), *French Women's Writing 1848–1994*, London & Atlantic Highlands, NJ, Athlone, 193–215.

Holmlund, Christine (1991), 'When is a lesbian not a lesbian?: the lesbian continuum and the mainstream *femme* film', *Camera Obscura*, 25–6: 144–79.

Hughes, David (1983), *The Sunday Times*, 16 October.

Kael, Pauline (1984), 'The current cinema: *Entre Nous*', *The New York Times*, 5 March.

Kaplan, E. Ann (1992), *Motherhood and Representation: The Mother in Popular Cinema and Melodrama*, London and New York, Routledge.

Manceaux, Michèle (1983), 'Diane Kurys: mon aventure-cinéma', *Marie Claire*, June.

Merck, Mandy (1986), '"Lianna" and the lesbians of art cinema', in Brunsdon, C. (ed.), *Films for Women*, London, BFI, 166–75.

Pascaud, François (1983), '*Coup de foudre*', *Télérama*, 13 March.

Perez, Michel (1983), '*Coup de foudre* de Diane Kurys: la subversion dans l'innocence', *Le Matin*, 9 April.

Portuges, Catherine (1988), 'Seeing subjects: women directors and cinematic autobiography', in Brodzki, B. and Schenck, C., *Life/Lines: Theorizing Women's Autobiography*, Ithaca and London, Cornell University Press, 338–50.

Powrie, Phil (1988), '*Coup de foudre*: nostalgia and lesbianism', *French Cinema in the 1980s*, Oxford, Oxford University Press, 62–74.

Quart, Barbara (1984), '*Entre Nous, a question of silence*', *Cinéaste*, 13: 3, 45–7.

Ross, Kristin (1995), *Fast Cars, Clean Bodies: Decolonization and the Reordering of French Culture*, Cambridge, Massachusetts and London, MIT Press.

Rochereau, Jean (1983), '*Coup de foudre* de Diane Kurys, Féminisme bien tempéré', *La Croix*, 7 June.

Straayer, Chris (1990), 'The hypothetical lesbian heroine', *Jump Cut*, 35, 50–7.

Tranchant, Marie-Noëlle (1983), 'Au bonheur de Diane', *Le Figaro*, 6 April.

Vincendeau, Ginette (1995), 'Unsettling memories', *Sight & Sound*, 5: 7, 30–2.

Walters, Suzanna Danuta (1992), *Lives Together/Worlds Apart, Mothers and Daughters in Popular Culture*, Berkeley, Los Angeles, Oxford, University of California Press.

4

Un homme amoureux

After the international success of *Coup de foudre*, Kurys turned
down Warner Brothers' proposal for an English-language remake
in favour of a project which, theoretically at least, would enable
her to get away from her personal life history, namely, a
contemporary love story inspired by fantasy rather than fact, set in
the privileged but (to her) familiar world of cinema. Whereas her
first three films had been closely tied in with a realistically
portrayed French social context, she wanted to give *Un homme
amoureux* an international perspective, focusing eventually on the
portrait of an American star making a film in Italy who falls in
love with a young French actress. To give the hero more weight,
she decided to base his starring role in the film within the film on
the life of a writer. She opted for the Italian Communist writer,
Cesare Pavese, because of 'l'énorme matière d'amour et de
douleur que charrient ses livres, par son impuissance, par son
obsession de la mort qu'il disait son "vice absurde"'[1] (Leclère
1987). Seemingly unaware of other European attempts to break
into the international (American) market, she told *Le Monde*, 'j'ai
décidé de tenter un pari: la création d'un nouveau genre cinéma-
tographique qui marierait un sujet français avec une distribution
internationale et un héros américain, un genre qu'on pourrait

---

1 'The enormous weight of love and pain which informs his books, his
impotence, and the obsession with death which he called his "absurd vice".'

baptiser "mid-Atlantique"'[2] (Braudau 1987). *Un homme amoureux*
is of particular interest in Kurys' *œuvre* as a self-reflexive film
which, in addition to its significance as a modern romance,
tackles, albeit obliquely and ambivalently, the position of women
within the cinema industry. Its charting of the emergence of a
young woman from bit-part actress to screenwriter follows the
route taken by Kurys herself in the 1970s. But Kurys' treatment of
her material makes the film problematic, precisely because it can
be dismissed as just a bland and glossy mid-Atlantic movie.

Un homme amoureux took two years to write. Kurys worked her
way through eight versions of the screenplay, spending several
months in the Midi with her old friend and co-writer Olivier
Schatzky. She also had to struggle to get funding for the film when
her American backers decided that the project was too European
and baroque (films about cinema are often not commercially
successful and the references to Pavese may have been thought to
bring bad luck). Fortunately, Michel Seydoux of Camera One
agreed to back her and supply the 35 million francs needed. Kurys
secured the use of Cinecittà, filming next door to Ettore Scola,
Luigi Comencini and Federico Fellini (who turned down her
request to make a brief cameo appearance). She recruited Dean
Tavoularis, Francis Ford Coppola's artistic director, to her technical
team and cast Peter Coyote and Greta Scacchi in the principal
roles with a supporting cast including Claudia Cardinale, Peter
Riegert, Vincent Lindon and Jamie Lee Curtis (who had adored
Coup de foudre). *Un homme amoureux* thus ended up as a Franco-
Italian co-production with an international cast, set amid sump-
tuous decors in Rome, Tuscany and Paris, and shot in Cinemascope and Dolby sound with an American artistic director. It was
made primarily in English and later dubbed in French for French
audiences, with Pierre Arditi speaking Peter Coyote's lines. It was
chosen to open the fortieth Cannes Film Festival in 1987 (in the
first version of the scenario, the film within the film was given a
gala presentation at Cannes!). However, it met with a divided

2 'I've decided to take a gamble: the creation of a new cinematic genre combining
  a French topic with an international cast and an American hero, a genre you
  could call "mid-Atlantic".'

critical response and was less successful at the box office than *Coup de foudre*. In many ways the film is a victim of its own ambitions, trying to pursue too many themes (the love affair, the film within the film, the ramifications of the love affair on the lives of others) and trying to please too many spectators (through its glamorous characters and glossy imagery), while failing to satisfy the expectations of spectators anticipating another woman-centred film.

Unlike her first three films, *Un homme amoureux* does not have a dedication or afterword to mark Kurys' autobiographical or authorial presence. Instead, the final shot of its central protagonist, un actress, sitting down to type out a manuscript entitled 'Un homme amoureux', constitutes a *mise en abîme* of the film as a whole, a device which once again invites the audience to question the status of what had appeared to be a third-person narrative, and to identify the role of the central protagonist with that of Kurys herself. Kurys clearly drew on her own career for her inspiration for the role: she, too, had worked in the theatre and in television in Paris and had had a bit part in a film being made in Rome (Fellini's *Casanova*, made in 1976, starring Donald Sutherland); and it was in Rome that she wrote an article on the shooting of the film for *Libération*. Signs of Kury's authorial signature are also to be found in the structural and thematic continuities between *Un homme amoureux* and the earlier films. It recalls the triangular relationships of *Cocktail Molotov* (the actress' lover even has the same name as Fred's friend, Bruno); and it reworks the problematic relationships between daughter, mother, and father, this time at a later stage in the daughter's life, the mother's role being once again directly inspired by Kurys' mother. Whatever Kurys' original intention, then, the finished film can be read in terms of the psychodrama of its implied author–director which gives the fantasised love story its particular inflection.

The narrative structure of *Un homme amoureux* is the most ambitious of all Kurys' films. It embeds the story of the filming of Cesare Pavese's last love affair and suicide in 1950 into a parallel love affair between the young Anglo-Italo-French actress, Jane Steiner (Greta Scacchi), and the film's American star, Steve Elliott (Peter Coyote), who plays Pavese to Jane's Gabriella, aided and abetted by his personal assistant, Michael (Peter Riegert). The progress of the affair is complicated by Jane's relationship with her live-in lover Bruno (Vincent Lindon), an avant-garde Parisian theatre director, and Steve's attachment to his American wife Susan (Jamie Lee Curtis), a former actress, and to his young children. It is further complicated by Jane's relationship with her dying mother, Julia (Claudia Cardinale), and her father, Harry (John Berry). When Jane meets Steve on the set of the Pavese film at Cinecittà in Rome, they are immediately attracted to one another. However, their relationship is not consummated until after Jane's role as Gabriella is over, when Steve suddenly walks out on Susan to spend a clandestine weekend with her in Paris, and Jane walks out on Bruno and her theatre friends. Steve has to return to Rome, but Jane's mother advises her daughter to make the most of the relationship, and when Steve then invites her back to his villa in Rome, Jane accepts. A period of romantic passion follows and Jane rejects Bruno when he tries to reclaim her; but when Susan returns unexpectedly to Rome, Jane is bundled out of the back door by Michael. The end of the affair is distressing for both Jane and Steve, and coincides with Steve's filming of Pavese's suicide and the death of Jane's mother. Steve spends a last night with Jane to comfort her, and Jane discovers her vocation as a writer. Though their affair has no future, it provides Jane with material for her writing. The final scene frames Jane, alone on the veranda of her parents' villa, starting to type the manuscript of 'Un homme amoureux', as the camera zooms out for the closing credits.

This plot outline leaves out of account the fragmented narrative of the making of the film about Pavese and the even more fragmented narrative of the film within the film about Pavese's last days, particularly his relationship with Gabriella. *Un homme amoureux* thus plays with a three-layered plot which is further complicated by the implication of the title of Jane's manuscript, 'Un homme amoureux', that the whole film can be read retrospectively as the representation of her screenplay. This device throws into question not just the chronology of the diegesis (events should be read as having taken place in the past rather than in the present) but also the status of those events (the subjective product of Jane's – or Kurys' – writing rather than an apparently objective third-person narration). In so doing, it points to an ambivalence about the 'real' subject of the film, which Kurys' own contradictory statements in the film's publicity brochure do nothing to assuage. Is *Un homme amoureux* about a man in love, 'ce qui se passe dans la tête et dans le cœur d'un acteur amoureux ...'[3] or is it '... l'histoire d'une femme qui rêve à un homme qui rêve à une femme qui rêve à ...'[4] (Kurys 1987)? The film initially cuts between the different characters without privileging any one particular viewpoint, but the introduction of Jane's voice-over some three-quarters of the way through the narrative effectively marginalises Steve's role from that point onwards. The voice-over charts the development of Jane's deepest (if superficially expressed) emotions, which are linked with her development as a writer: first, her feelings about Steve which she writes down as she is waiting for him at the villa, then her separation from Steve and memory of their argument about whether or not it is possible to love more than one person, then her love for her mother as she looks at her during their last dinner party together, and finally her acknowledgement of her debt to her mother as she starts writing her screenplay, 'Julia's strength was within me – all at once I knew I was going to confront my life as she had confronted her death ...'. Just as the film's title turns out to refer to Jane's manuscript rather than to Steve as subject, so Jane's voice-over works belatedly to confirm that the 'real' subject of the film is Jane.

Not surprisingly, one of the major criticisms made about the film was that the overlong and convoluted plot lacked coherence and rhythm. The spectator is expected to follow too many threads, none of which are dealt with adequately. Key secondary characters – Bruno, Julia, Harry, Susan – appear intermittently and irregularly within the narrative, their scenes often abruptly inserted into the narrative of Steve and Jane, their existence otherwise ignored. Despite the apparent significance of the lines Steve speaks when

3 'what goes on in the head and the heart of an actor in love'.
4 '... the story of a woman who dreams of a man who dreams of a woman who dreams of ...'

thinking about or performing Pavese, the focus on the film-making process in the first half of the film fades away as the love affair takes over in importance, undermining the interest of the film within the film. Indeed, the business and complexity of the subplots do not mask the fact that they serve primarily as exotic backdrop to the impossible love affair between Steve and Jane, the course of which many critics dismissed in terms normally reserved for fiction written by and/or for women, like 'de la guimauve', 'un photo roman', 'une bluette sentimentale'⁵ or 'up-market Mills and Boonland'. However, the structure of *Un homme amoureux* refuses some of the pleasures typical of a Mills and Boon romance. Not only is Jane's status as heroine not fully acknow-ledged, there is no tension as to whether or not the romantic hero will succumb to her charms (Steve is struck from the first moment he sees her), and there is no possibility of a conventional happy ending (Steve will not leave his wife). Instead of capturing a man in love, the independent woman resigns herself to losing him and sets to work on the manuscript of 'A Man in Love' instead. A film with such an ending potentially offers alternative satisfactions to the romance, either through melodrama (and identification with the suffering of women in a patriarchal society) or through the emergence of the independent woman (and the pleasures of a critique of a patriarchal society). Yet the film both refuses the plenitude of identification with the central woman character and lacks an alternative ironic or critical perspective on her situation.

Unlike Kurys' first three films, the events of *Un homme amoureux* take place in a historical vacuum. Kurys argued that the artificial world of cinema was the ideal setting for romance, since 'pendant un tournage, dans l'ambiance bizarre d'un studio, [l'amour] est encore plus intense, plus fragile ...'⁶ (Kurys 1987). The glamorous settings chosen to give substance to the characters of the American star and the cosmopolitan European actress belong to the world of tourist brochures and glossy magazines rather than contemporary social reality. The opening credit

5 'slush', 'a photo romance', 'lightweight romantic fiction'.
6 'during shooting, in the curious atmosphere of a studio, [love] is even more intense and fragile ...'

sequence sets the tone with a montage of clichéd shots of Rome devoid of references to Cinecittà or the story to come. The spectator can then compare Jane's parents' villa with its views of the beautiful Tuscany countryside, Steve's villa in Rome with its gardens, pool and tennis court, and Jane and Bruno's comfortably Bohemian Parisian flat with its panoramic views over Paris. Steve and Jane's love scene in Paris takes place in an upmarket hotel bedroom, and is intercut with clichéd shots of the romantic couple on a bridge over the Seine. As Olivier Schmitt suggests, 'Ils font la tournée des "incontournables", un forfait culturel en somme'[7] (Schmitt 1986). The banality of the *mise-en-scène* is underscored by the theme of international travel (Susan twice flies in from New York, Steve's agent once, and Jane, her parents, Steve and Bruno at various times travel between Italy and Paris) and the film's visual texture is punctuated with shots of international phone calls, hotels and meetings in airports. Bad weather, like the rain in Rome and the thunderstorm in Tuscany, does not undermine the tourist imagery but simply gives outward expression to the feelings of the heart, like waiting for the dawn, another clichéd image which the film uses twice.

An important element of the *mise-en-scène* is the representation of the Cinecittà film studios and the activity involved in making a film. The question here is whether *Un homme amoureux* uses Cinecittà as a glamorous backdrop to the development of the characters, or whether it permits any demystification of the filmmaking process. Kurys herself had become a filmmaker as a result of dissatisfaction with the roles she was given as an actress, and the siting of her film in the world of cinema suggests the possibility of incorporating a woman's critical point of view. However, though Jane is critical of aspects of what she sees (she walks out when the studio manager tries to have her drunken father thrown off the set), her role is that of the privileged outsider spending three days with the stars. The camera accompanies her arrival at Cinecittà in time to witness the end of a scene of the Pavese film being shot, the set of which is the exterior of the Hotel

7 'They see all the principal sights, it's a cultural tour, basically.'

Roma in Turin, complete with period Lancia car.[8] Jane's first sight
of the studio and set coincides with her first sight of Steve, a
privileged moment which Kurys organises with consummate
skill, using a long take which involves complicated interactions
between the foreground (the studio floor and the film crew) and
the background (the set), in which the camera pans to follow
Steve's movements until he is in the same frame as Jane, sees her
and writes the name Gabriella on the glass of the phone booth.
Subsequent shots allow the spectator to follow Jane behind the
scenes to view the costumes department, the studio canteen
outside which child actors are wandering around in costume, and
the dressing rooms. The film thus uses Jane to present the (male)
star and the studios from the point of view of a fascinated (female)
fan, rather than providing a critical purchase on a male-dominated
institution.

However, the *mise-en-scène* of the film within a film is also used
in a more self-conscious way to blur the distinctions between
appearance and reality. On one level Kurys simply depicts the
apparatus of filmmaking (including shots of the director and
crew, the clapper-board, the studio set with its missing fourth
wall, actors on set waiting for shooting to begin, etc.). But at times
she cuts directly to shots belonging to the film within the film,
then reveals their status through devices like the sound of a
whistle or the shout of 'Cut' or the entry of non-actors onto the set.
These moments may be unsettling in the way they call into
question the spectator's ability to distinguish when an actor is
'acting' and his or her 'real' feelings. For example, the spectator
(like Jane) is shocked when Steve walks away from her with
apparent indifference after he has been trying to woo her as
Gabriella. The distinction between appearance and reality is
further blurred in the seduction scene where Pavese/Steve falls
sobbing onto the body of Gabriella/Jane and is disturbed later by
Jane's unscheduled appearance on set, playfully dressed as a
prostitute in period costume. Towards the end of the film, Steve's
entrance into a hotel in a state of distress leads to confusion as to

8 The Lancia is a fetish car of Marguerite Duras' novels and Jane's name, Steiner,
  recalls the series of short films by Duras entitled *Aurélia Steiner* (1979).

whether it is Steve or Pavese who is about to commit suicide. However, the film's play with the spectator's desire to be taken in by appearances is not consistent. Kurys 'cheats' in the outdoor dance scene where Pavese first meets Gabriella by using an already edited sequence in a scene which is supposed to be being filmed 'live'. But in any case, the film within the film allows only one layer of illusion to be peeled away, revealing the 'reality' constructed by the framing film, that is the relationship between Steve and Jane. It does not call into question the 'reality' of the film being made by Kurys (except through its ending), it does not foreground the ideological work of film (there is no explicit critique of the way Pavese and Gabriella are being represented) and it does not even foreground acting as work (Jane is not seen preparing the role of Gabriella, and Steve's problems with his role simply reinforce the star's moody and sensitive persona). The *mise-en-scène* of the film within the film works as exotic local colour for the romance story rather than making a meaningful statement about the filmmaking process.

The lack of critical edge in the *mise-en-scène* is confirmed by the handling of the soundtrack. Georges Delerue's extravagant, swelling strings produce 'flonflons d'une musique particulièrement guimauve'[9] (Macia and Baron 1987) which accompany the film from the opening credit sequence through to the final credits. The intrusive music crudely underlines every stage of the affair between Steve and Jane, their encounters with solitude and with death, and the development of Jane's subjective voice-over. The only relief from it lies in the diegetic dance music, used for the meeting between Pavese and Gabriella and for the scene in Steve's dressing-room where Steve and Jane dance to the sound of a period record-player surmounted by tiny dancing figures, and in the intense silence that accompanies their first love-making scene. The lack of subtlety and poignancy of the incidental music is matched by the film's use of multiple languages. English dominates the film due to the central role of Steve, but it sounds

9 'particularly slushy musical refrains'. (Georges Delerue was the composer for nine of Truffaut's films.)

artificial and wooden, even as spoken by native speakers. Greta Scacchi in particular seems unable to breathe life into her script, or even to differentiate the sound of screaming from laughing. The switching between English, French and Italian often seems gratuitous and pretentious, while the decision to show the Italians making a film in English about Pavese, speaking broken English at a press conference, and speaking English on set because of their American star, though it could be read as a comment on the state of the film industry in Italy, is also readable simply as part of Kurys' bid for an international (American) audience for *Un homme amoureux*.

If the function of the filmmaking scenes within the film is mainly to provide local colour, the choice of Pavese as the subject of the film within the film begs some questions about the way Pavese functions as a source of meaning. Olivier Shatsky, Kurys' co-writer, described the need to 'assurer, dans une période anti-intellectuelle, anti-gauche, la pérennité d'un intellectuel aussi fascinant que Pavese, le poète et l'homme de gauche politiquement engagé'[10] (Schmitt 1986). Kurys herself, however, was clear that the film was not about Pavese (a topic for the Italian film industry) but that the representation of Pavese gave substance to the character of Steve. Steve's star quality is initially constructed through his passionate defence of the Pavese project at the press conference which opens the diegesis. He recounts his fascination with the 'commie' writer and poet who is unknown in the United States and, more particularly, the moment when, after meeting a young woman, Pavese decides to stop writing and, on 27 August 1950, aged forty-two, takes an overdose of sleeping tablets. Shots of the Pavese film within the film subsequently focus on the writer's last days, his meeting with Gabriella, his tortured attempt to make love to her and his suicide. So the film makes no attempt to address the complexities of Pavese as novelist, poet, publisher, translator and political exile under Mussolini. Typical of Kurys' style, Pavese's political views have to be inferred from the use of

10 'ensure, in an anti-intellectual, anti-leftwing period, the perennial importance of an intellectual as fascinating as Pavese, the poet and committed leftwing activist'.

Communist party posters in the *mise-en-scène*. In fact, Kurys' choice of Pavese as the topic of the film within the film, a film which is being directed by a director, Pizani (Jean Pigozzi), who comes, like Kurys, from the theatre, works in a rather self-congratulatory way to validate the European film industry (and hence Kurys herself) for taking on a worthwhile but non-profit-making topic. It is notable that Steve refuses to cancel the project to take up an option with Warner Bros. Furthermore, the incorporation of Pavese's reflections on creativity, solitude and death enable some uneasy parallels to be drawn, not just between Pavese and Steve, but also between Pavese and Jane, who discovers her vocation as a writer in the course of the film, and thus, by extension, between Pavese and Kurys, the screenwriter, herself.

Steve, the ostensible subject of the film, is constructed not just through his identification with Pavese, but through scenes which depict his lifestyle as an American star on location in Italy. The rented villa and Mercedes, the visits from his wife and children and from his agent, the support provided by his assistant Michael, his disagreements with Pizani over his role, his moodiness on set and at home, his inability to sleep, his occasionally childish, capricious behaviour, are all signs of the way he functions as star, a function which is attested to in public by scenes such as the press conference, the young female fans gathered around his car, his anger at an unauthorised photographer. His privileged and protected lifestyle is best understood through his relationships with Michael and Susan. Michael, his good-humoured buddy and confidante, once a kosher butcher in New York, now 'Steve's slave', attends to Steve's every whim, entertains him and Jane, clears up after him, and endures his abuse. Susan, the apparently hysterical wife, is actually an attractive, intelligent woman, a former actress who is committed to her husband, tolerant of his moodiness and able to manage him just like she manages the studio bosses. Though her marriage is threatened by Steve's confession about his affair with Jane, Susan is last seen putting her clothes away instead of leaving. Her phone calls to Steve punctuate his relationship with Jane, as do Steve's loving stories about his seven-year-old son. Because of the way Michael and

Susan protect Steve from the real world, there is a danger of him emerging as an irresponsible, superficial character. His investment in the role of Pavese and the parallel between Pavese's suicidal despair and his own doomed affair with Jane give his character a spurious depth and seriousness which would otherwise be lacking.

Steve's commitment to the Pavese role initially confers upon him the status of subject of the film. His physical similarity to Pavese is established through the similarity of their dress codes, Steve's shirts and dark glasses matching Pavese's crisp short-sleeved white shirts and period glasses, the mark of the intellectual. Steve's fascination with Jane is enhanced by their acting out of the first encounters between Pavese and Gabriella, and is cemented when Steve gives Jane a copy of Pavese's diary (about 'the pain of living') and they watch the dawn rise after spending the night wandering the streets of Rome together. During the next day's shooting, Steve holds Jane in his arms in his dressing-room before the scene in which he tries and fails to make love with Gabriella and that evening, Jane's last evening in Rome, he invites her back to his villa but is unable to make love to her because of her panic reaction to the 'grass' they have been smoking. The parallel with Pavese then ceases, since Steve pursues Jane to Paris, successfully consummates their relationship, and eventually installs her in his villa in Rome, with few signs of guilt or torment about his betrayal of Susan. However, reality intrudes when a photographer takes an illicit photograph of them kissing on set (one of a series of photos which mark Jane's narrative progress from object to subject). Steve becomes violent and abusive, damages his car in an aggressive car chase on the studio lot, and bawls out Michael, a sign of the underlying tensions and anxieties provoked by his situation. For though he claims that it is possible to love more than one person at once, he is unable to live out this situation in practice. When Susan returns and Steve lets Jane go, his depression mirrors that of Pavese and the film tricks the spectator into thinking that Steve, too, may be contemplating suicide. However, Steve is not of the same calibre as Pavese, according to whom, 'One does not kill oneself for the love of a woman, but because love – any love – reveals in us all our nakedness, our misery, our vulnerability, our void ...' Steve's void is revealed by his lack of commitment, which is only partially redeemed by his response to Jane's call for help after the death of her mother. By this point, however, he has already become a marginalised, distant figure.

Jane, in contrast, lives her (admittedly privileged) life openly and honestly. An attractive young woman, her ordinary, everyday clothes (jeans and shirts) express her unspoiled simplicity while her defence of her father's right to solicit an interview with Steve and her refusal to hide what she is doing from Bruno demonstrate her strength of character. She believes in her right to new sexual and emotional experiences, even if it involves a doomed affair with a famous married man, and she pursues her desires without guilt or shame. She returns Steve's gaze when she sees him in the studio and she responds actively to his attempts to seduce her; when Steve returns to Rome, she takes the initiative and calls him; when her mother dies, she calls him again and expresses her need for him. The emotional crisis she goes through is ultimately more devastating than Steve's for she loses both a lover and a mother. Indeed, her excess of grief at the 'real' death of her mother contrasts with Steve's investment in the death of Pavese which is faked and artificial. But she is also able to learn from her experiences and, whereas Steve (presumably) returns to his familiar contained world, Jane takes over Pavese's place both as writer and as subject of the film. Jane's function as the active agent of her sexual and emotional desire gives the lie to Kurys' affirmation that, 'Un homme amoureux, cela a plus de sens qu'une femme amoureuse parce que l'amour rend l'homme actif tandis que les femmes – c'est le cas du rôle de Greta Scacchi – sont générale-ment plus passives ...'[11] (Ferenczi 1987).

However, the same cannot be said of Jane's role as Gabriella, which is more typical of conventional cinematic roles for women. Gabriella, as directed by Pizani, is a provocative, self-centred creature with a coy little (English) voice, whose role is little more

11 'A man in love makes more sense than a woman in love because love makes a man active while women – as in Greta Scacchi's role – are generally more passive ...'

than a decorative foil to the representation of the older, tormented male writer. Gabriella's own feelings, history and sexuality are of no interest in themselves, even to Jane. Jane happily submits to playing a pastiche of 1950s fetishised femininity, shot in glorious technicolour makeup and revealing costumes, displaying her breasts and corsets in the face of her lover's physical advances. There are no scenes which directly critique the marginality of Gabriella's role or the exploitative way in which it is filmed. After the tormented sex scene between Pavese and Gabriella, when Jane is ignored and Steve acclaimed with reverence, the difference in the way they are treated can be attributed to differences between the unknown actor and the star rather than to gender difference. However, the moment when Jane poses as a prostitute on the set of a scene Steve is shooting is potentially more disruptive. The scene punctures the seriousness of the (male) director and earns her his wrath because it distracts Steve away from his job. But it also indirectly invites the spectator to contrast Jane's active intervention in the Steve/Pavese narrative (she runs off set with him) with her passive playing of Gabriella, a contrast which the film otherwise refuses to spell out.

Jane's indifference to Gabriella can be read as typical both of Kurys' refusal of a wholeheartedly woman-centred perspective and of the character's detachment and self-absorption which emerges most fully from the final scene in which she starts to write. Jane's ultimate solitude is never really in question and is most fully expressed in the shot at Rome airport where she is framed behind the plate-glass window looking down on the arrival of Steve's family. Her commitment to Steve and belief in their relationship is questionable, given her mother's advice to use the affair as the basis for future memories. Her relationship with Steve is characterised as much by detached observation as by stormy passion, whether it is expressed through the construction of Steve as the object of desire, through the sex scenes or through what Jane has to say (or write) about him. Steve is regularly shot from Jane's point of view, from the scene where she first sees him in the studio (trapped within the phone box on the phone to his wife), to the scene in his dressing-room (where he is also on the phone to Susan), to his arrival in Paris in the auditorium of the theatre where she is rehearsing with Bruno. As Georgiana Colvile (1993) points out, Peter Coyote's long, lean face, dark hair and brooding sensuality conforms to a physical type favoured by a number of French women directors. However, if Steve is the object of Jane's desire, he is also ultimately unattainable, contrary to the conventions of the romance.

Furthermore, the sex scenes of *Un homme amoureux* do not follow through the focus on Jane's point of view. Kurys wanted them to be different from conventional cinematic sex scenes and spent some time researching what made sex scenes in other films powerful. As a result, the first moments of the first love scene between Jane and Steve, shot in silence as they stand together with her back against a wall, produce what Marcia Pally (1987) calls 'a first rate job with the slow release of sexual tension', achieved, not through showing the sex act itself, but through focusing on the actors' breathing and expressions. Their mutual desire and pleasure contrasts favourably with the sex scene between Gabriella and Pavese, where Jane/Gabriella looks on fearfully as the shot foregrounds Steve/Pavese and his anguished need and desire. Hints at male impotence and a shot of Jane reaching down to caress herself in a subsequent sex scene call attention to the question of women's sexual pleasure, already raised in *Cocktail Molotov* and *Coup de foudre*. However, Colvile's claim that in one scene Steve and Jane achieve orgasm 'par le biais du récit rituel que fait celle-ci, de son initiation primitive par sa mère'[12] (Colvile 1993: 79) is not borne out by the dialogue. Although, as Judith Mayne argues (1990: 126), 'a fantasy of lesbian lovemaking' is invoked, it is clear from Jane's response to Steve's prompts and corrections that the fantasy in question is his. Other aspects of the way the sex scenes are shot are even more problematic. Many critics saw the film as simply providing tasteful but banal displays of Scacchi's near perfect body which is fetishised through a number of insert close-ups of her buttocks or shots of her undressing without there being comparable shots of Coyote. The

12 'through Jane's ritual narration of her early initiation by her mother'.

sex scenes, then, do not inscribe a woman's point of view, even if they do challenge certain other cinematic conventions.

However, the last night Jane and Steve spend together is of a rather different order. Steve lies on top of the grieving Jane in order to hold and comfort her rather than have sex. The scene marks the end of their relationship and of Steve's ability to give her what she needs, and it is after this that she is able to start writing seriously. Earlier, Jane had noted, when waiting for Steve to come home from the studio, that Steve's face in sleep 'looking like death' inspired her to probe within herself, 'peering inside of you to see what I am or what I think I'll be'. Later, from a foetal position on Steve's sofa, she had asked Steve whether or not she should have a baby, as though Steve's function were to help her work out her desires. At the end it is thanks to Steve (who gave her Pavese's diary), as well as her mother (whose perfume lingers on) and father (whose typewriter she appropriates), that Jane becomes a writer; and the new Jane, the lonely writer now rich in memories, sets out to incorporate her past experiences into her work. But an insert of a photograph of Jane as a child in the final sequence reveals, tellingly, that the real focus of Jane's project is the representation of the self.

In *Un homme amoureux*, Kurys creates a fantasised nuclear family in which the marital breakup represented in her first three films has been redeemed (the mother has let the father come back into her life) and the only daughter is the sole object of her parents' love. Jane describes her mother as a strong independent-minded woman who left her husband, taking her daughter with her, in order to run an art gallery in Paris. The father rejoined them later, unable to bear the separation. The film does not show signs of Julia's professional past, instead she is positioned within the home as the idealised, perfect mother, still beautiful and attractive to men but also available for her loving daughter whom she encourages to experience life to the full. The compatibility between mother and daughter is based (unusually) on their shared love of life, their independence, and their refusal of the conventional. In the film's publicity brochure, Kurys describes the mother figure as being the heart of the story. Certainly a mother figure who is independent, positive and blameless is a rarity, even in feminist fictions, which tend to hold the mother responsible for the way the daughter gets socialised into patriarchal society. Fictional daughters are often only able to make their peace with the mother after the mother's death and it is significant, therefore, that the film ends positively with the daughter's return to the mother's space before she dies. The two-shots of Julia and Jane hugging in the grounds of their Tuscan villa are the warmest shots in the film, and during their last dinner party together Jane's voice-over describes the 'certain look we'd always shared ... Never again would anyone listen to me with that kind of attention ... I didn't want her to leave me alone ...', as the image track cuts between Jane looking and the mother as the object of her loving gaze.

But even in this expression of love, Jane's concern is as much about herself as about her mother. The theme of the mother's terminal illness (echoing references to illness in *Diabolo menthe* and *Cocktail Molotov*) is revived as a narrative strand only when Jane's idyll with Steve is over when, arguably, it works to empower Jane and disempower Julia. Julia feels obliged to confess her sins, namely that she lied about abandoning Chico, the family dog (a motif which is taken up in *La Baule Les Pins*), and she becomes dependent on Jane for being put out of her pain. The film does not show her death, instead the camera discreetly pans over a table laden with books labelled as gifts. But the effect is to foreground the daughter's grief and the way in which the experience allows her to grow. After her last night with Steve, Jane says, 'Steve left next morning ... I'd never felt quite so alone ... All at once I realised that Julia's strength was within me, that I knew I was going to confront my life as she had confronted her death ... That year I stayed at the house and wrote until winter – my mother's perfume still lingered in her room.' The mother's death is important, not so much in itself, but because it allows the daughter to become a strong, independent, creative woman.

Un homme amoureux also plays with Kurys' dream of being reunited with the father, though Harry appears only intermittently within the film and is an ambivalent figure. Despite his

Jewish name (Steiner), his apparently American (mid-Atlantic?) accent, and his past as a journalist with the BBC, the film makes nothing of his ethnicity or past history. Instead he is depicted as a loving but faintly ridiculous, ineffectual, pathetic figure, who has taken to drink and whose work now consists of writing articles for airline magazines on topics like what the Pope has for lunch. His function in the plot lies in securing Steve's interest in Jane by appearing drunk on the set of the Pavese film hoping for an interview with Steve. Jane finds his presence embarrassing and hesitates between ignoring him and defending him, but she eventually assumes her responsibilities, takes the studio to task for their treatment of him and walks out on the film as a matter of principle. By so doing, she shows Steve that she is not just a physically attractive woman, but also his equal, someone who cares about her family and who acts on principle. Thereafter the father's role is marginalised and the last shot of him, sitting outside the villa in the rain to nurse his grief over Julia's death, shows that he is ultimately unable to provide Jane with the comfort she needs. Instead, the film ends with Jane sitting at his typewriter, in the place at the table which he had occupied at the beginning of the film, starting work on her manuscript. The inserted close-up of the title of her manuscript, 'Un homme amoureux', not only shows that she has taken her father's place but also that what she has to say is (presumably) superior to anything that he has written. Like the mother, and like Steve, too, the father has been successfully incorporated and dispatched.

Jane's relationships with others outside of the family are also problematic. She is unable (or unwilling) to make a success of her relationship with Bruno, even though Bruno, too, is a successful, creative artist (an actor in and director of a production of *La Veillée* by Jérôme Deschamps and Macha Makeieff). Bruno has something of the spontaneity, humour, sensitivity and lack of respect for convention which characterised the Bruno of *Cocktail Molotov*. But he is more like a friend than a lover and there are no scenes of passion between him and Jane. Though his answering-machine recording refers to them as 'Jane and Tarzan', he is not a Tarzan-like figure. Indeed, though he becomes insolent and aggressive in response to Steve's presence in La Coupole, his reaction amounts to deliberately dribbling wine down his own shirt. He is unable to persuade Jane not to leave him to join Steve and when he turns up in Rome, a lonely, pathetic figure, the camera stays with Jane as she declines to return to Paris with him. Jane's inability to commit herself to the loving but inadequate Bruno is matched by her lack of relationships with women of her own generation. She has no sister and no girlfriend and feels no complicity with Susan except inasmuch as she speculates that if Steve can leave Susan, he can leave her too. Susan, the wife, is represented as a jealous rival, dependent on a man to give her life meaning, leaving the independent Jane to occupy the centre of the frame in splendid isolation.

Un homme amoureux is potentially a fascinating film in the way it weaves a melodramatic love story into a cinematic setting, focalised through a woman's point of view. In her use of the film within the film, Kurys challenges male domination of the genre, not so much reworking self-reflexive *auteur* films such as Godard's *Le Mépris* (1963) and Truffaut's *La Nuit américaine* (1973) (though the film's ambivalent ending does suggest a *mise en abîme* of the filmmaking process) as evoking 1950s Hollywood melodramas about filmmaking like *Singin' in the Rain* (Stanley Donen 1952), *A Star is Born* (George Cukor 1954), *The Barefoot Contessa* (Joseph Mankiewicz 1954) and *Two Weeks in Another Town* (Vincente Minnelli 1962). (The casting of Cardinale is also evocative of films of the 1950s and 1960s.) In *Un homme amoureux*, the small part actress has no ambition to dominate the screen of the film she is making (there is no sense of her going on to bigger and better parts), her part is significant only inasmuch as it allows her access to a relationship with Steve. But the way the narrative is eventually focalised through her point of view invites comparison with the spectacular Hollywood women's pictures of the 1950s. However, *Un homme amoureux* fails to offer the traditional pleasures of the woman's picture, since Kurys refuses the full potential of Jane's role as subject and narrator. The film does not open with Jane's concerns or develop coherently from Jane's point of view, but only allows her to be seen as its subject retrospectively; and it does not function to reconcile the contra-dictions of a woman's role within a patriarchal society, since Jane operates as a free agent, unfettered by conventional moral codes. Her desire for Steve is hardly transgressive in the privileged Bohemian circles in which she moves, the loss of Bruno causes her little pain and she accepts from the beginning that her affair with Steve has no future. Though Jane may grieve at the end for the loss of Steve and the death of her mother, she is hardly a victim of the patriarchal order and her transformation into a writer, as the swelling music recognises, is not exactly a cause for tears.[13] In the end, then, *Un homme amoureux* is a rather hollow film, which fails to move cinema audiences like the 1950s women's films which it evokes.

References

Braudau, Michel (1987), '*Un homme amoureux* de Diane Kurys, le poids des sentiments', *Le Monde*, 9 May.

Colvile, Georgiana (1993), 'Mais qu'est-ce qu'elles voient? Regards de Françaises à la caméra', *The French Review*, 67: 1.

Ferenczi, Aurélien (1987), 'Diane Kurys: mon sujet s'est construit en cours de tournage', *Quotidien de Paris*, 7 May.

Kurys, Diane (1987), *Un homme amoureux*, publicity brochure.

Leclère, Marie-Françoise (1987), 'Kurys: le miroir de Diane', *Le Point*, 763, 4 May.

Macia, Jean-Luc and Baron, Jeanine (1987), '*Un homme amoureux* de Diane Kurys, grands sentiments à petits pas', *La Croix*, 11 May.

Mayne, Judith (1990), *The Woman at the Keyhole: Feminism and Women's Cinema*, Bloomington and Indianapolis, Indiana University Press.

Pally, Marcia (1987), 'Kurys makes her bed', *Film Comment*, 23: 5.

Schmitt, Olivier (1986), 'Diane Kurys tourne à Rome, le rêve américain', *Le Monde*, 6 November.

13 In Jean-Jacques Annaud's 1991 film of *The Lover* by Marguerite Duras, the woman writer is similarly figured through the fetichised opening image of the woman at a typewriter.

5

La Baule Les Pins

Kurys' response to the disappointing critical reception of *Un homme amoureux* was to set aside plans for making another grandiose love story (to be shot in English and set in Czechoslovakia and Poland in the immediate postwar period) in favour of a more intimate drama about childhood in France. After struggling with ideas for a film with a contemporary setting, she turned back to the period of her own childhood and allowed memories of the past to take over: 'tout s'est débloqué: les anecdotes, les souvenirs, les images sont revenues ... Et ... j'ai "accouché" du sujet!'[1] (Kurys 1990). Originally conceived as a film in which the only characters would be children, Kurys eventually introduced the adults' drama of marital break-up in counterpoint. Consequently the film is not just about 'what it feels like to be a child, to have cousins and a big sister, not to be able to do your shoelaces up', it is also about 'what it's like to sense a drama taking place around you without fully understanding it' (Vincendeau 1991: 69–70). She wrote the screenplay for *La Baule Les Pins* with her collaborator on *Coup de foudre*, Alain Le Henry, in a month, 'il est sorti de mon imagination comme un spoutnik'[2] (Pantel 1989), without apparently realising the extent to which it takes up and reworks the settings and themes of *Diabolo menthe* and *Coup de foudre*. It took a mere three months to put together the production

1 'It all came unblocked: stories, memories, images came back to me ... And ... I gave birth to the film.'
2 'It came out of my imagination like a sputnik.'

money and distribution arrangements, she engaged a star-studded French cast including Nathalie Baye, Richard Berry, Zabou and Jean-Pierre Bacri, and the film was shot on location in Cinemascope in the Autumn of 1989. When it came out, in February 1990, it was well received, even by Kurys' family (who did not find it particularly true to their own memories of the period). However, the return to the autobiographical raw material of her two previous hits, growing up female and the break-up of her parents' marriage, points to the obsessiveness of Kurys' preoccupations and begs the question as to whether another film can provide new insights and pleasures. *La Baule Les Pins* reproduces the splitting of sympathy and identification between the adult woman's need for independence and the husband and children's insecurity and loss. But the different inflections of the story and the gorgeous reconstruction of the small seaside town of La Baule Les Pins in the summer of 1958 suggest that the forcefulness of *Coup de foudre* may have been attenuated by a more nostalgic, less subversive revisioning of the past.

Like *Un homme amoureux*, *La Baule Les Pins* does not use a dedication or afterword to signal Kurys' authorial presence, but instead develops the use of the subjective female voice-over. The events of the family summer holiday are focalised through the point of view of thirteen-year-old Frédérique (Julie Bataille), the elder daughter of Léna (Nathalie Baye) and Michel (Richard Berry). Extracts from Frédérique's secret diary punctuate the narrative and are used to introduce the characters, chart her relationship with her older cousin Daniel (Alexis Derlon) and express her anxieties about her parents and her future (Kurys herself recalls worrying whether she would ever see her dolls and her bedroom again). The diary signals Frédérique's isolation, since she has no other interlocutor. She dedicates it to 'an unknown friend' (the spectator?), uses it to hide her father's photograph, worries (or hopes?) that her mother will find it, and at one point wonders if she should address it to Daniel. However, at the end of the film her voice-over transcribes a mundane letter she has written to her father after the events of the film are over, asking about arrangements for the Christmas holidays. The switch from diary to letter and the acceptance of separation from the father are signs that she has left childish feelings behind and entered a more grown-up, if repressed, world. The film's ending thus marks a development of sorts from the stasis of the ending of *Coup de foudre*, showing that the daughter will survive, if at a cost. If Frédérique's voice-over provides a certain coherence to the progression of events in *La Baule Les Pins*, however, its fragmented use does not allow the spectator to identify fully with her point of view, and the ambivalence about who the diary is addressed to is symptomatic of Kurys' ambivalence about the audience for her films.

La Baule Les Pins opens with an establishing shot of Lyons and a pre-credit sequence set in the Korski household. Frédérique and the nanny, Odette (Valéria Bruni-Tedeschi), are packing for the summer holidays. Stubborn little Sophie (Candice Lefranc) refuses to put on her summer shoes, goes off in search of her mother for support, and catches sight of her parents having visibly just had a row, her father in tears. The sequence cuts to Léna accompanying her children to the train, but at the last moment telling them that she will not be going with them. The film then cuts to the credit sequence, an evocative montage of shots of a sunset, waves, the seashore, gulls and horses, and the villas of (presumably) La Baule Les Pins, accompanied by the nostalgic strains of The Platters singing 'Twilight Time'. The sequence invites spectators to invest the imaginary space of the seaside with their own memories, ending on a re-establishing shot of the bay as the sun sets. The bay then comes to life for the duration of the movie until the final credit sequence leaves spectators with a last long shot of the beach, seen this time from the perspective of the place once occupied by the two families whose lives they have shared, as the departing figures of Frédérique and the other children disappear from view. Compared with Kurys' earlier films, this moment of closure more obviously consigns the action of the film to a nostalgically-remembered past, which Frédérique's voice-over both confirms and disturbs. But the contrast between the despair and unhappiness of the fragmented pre-credit sequence and the aural and visual plenitude of the credit sequence sets up a tension between narrative and image which is exploited throughout the diegesis.

The narrative itself is divided between the experiences of the children and the drama taking place between the adults. The film explores the everyday activities and changing emotions of the two girls, who are thrown together for the holidays with their aunt Bella (Zabou) and their uncle Léon (Jean-Pierre Bacri), who are staying at a nearby villa with their children, Daniel, Suzanne, René and Titi. The girls are subjected to and rebel against the petty rules and regulations of the long-suffering Odette and their small-minded landlord, M. Ruffier (Didier Bénureau). The film progresses, like *Diabolo menthe*, through brief, well-observed, often humorous scenes, which evoke universal memories of childhood holidays and growing up. The summer-holiday setting creates a unity of time and place which allows time to be slowed down to the pace of the children's perceptions and multiple mini-storylines to be initiated and developed. For example, Titi eventually manages to tie up his shoelaces, M. Ruffier's goldfish die from the suppositories Frédérique and Sophie throw into his pond every night, the stray dog which attaches itself to Michel has to be abandoned. Many scenes foregrounding the children's activities could be inserted at any moment in the narrative, like naughty Sophie giving her cousin soap to eat instead of a sweet. But their activities have an impact on the adults' drama when their late return from an abortive expedition through the pines to find 'the house where they torture women', led by Daniel, means that Léna misses her last rendezvous with her lover Jean-Claude (Vincent Lindon). And their burning down of the Beach Club, after René is disqualified from winning the prize for best sandcastle for not being a member, stands out as a demonstration of their communal revolt against an unjust adult world.

The children's activities intersect with the more threatening scenes of the adults' emotional crises, experienced primarily from the children's point of view. The most dramatic narrative thread is the unfolding story of the parent's imminent separation, filtered through the gossiping of Odette and Bella and the diary entries of Frédérique, which erupts periodically into the image track. Léna leaves her children at the station in order to look for a job and a flat in Paris, and comes to La Baule only when she is required to mediate the hostility between Odette and the children, where she carries on her affair with Jean-Claude; she returns to Paris to continue her search and is therefore absent when Michel arrives and discovers Jean-Claude's proposal of marriage, written on a beer mat; when she comes back again in her newly purchased car, Michel smashes it up and then tries to strangle her, before becoming aware that a hysterical Frédérique is holding a shard of broken mirror to her throat and threatening to kill herself. The definitive break-up of the nuclear family is figured, as in *Coup de foudre*, through a fragmented sequence in which Léna tells Michel their marriage is over, a scene witnessed by the two daughters. The moments of crisis break with the rest of the film's visual style through their fragmented editing, which emphasises both the bitterness of the relationship between husband and wife and the emotional damage inflicted on the children. Multiple shots frame the children in windows or doorways, alone, helplessly watching, like the shot of Sophie pulling the head and limbs from her doll. However, the film also shows the girls' resilience and ability to survive, and in a sequence which serves as a coda to the rest of the film, Sophie performs a ballet dance at the last family gathering, a scene which matches Frédérique's letter to her father. As in Kurys' other films, writing and performance are ways of seeking parental love and approval but also compensate for its lack.

The fragmented sequences detailing the disintegration of the family are themselves compensated for, or at least held in tension with, the more obviously reliable pleasures of the film's otherwise detailed, sparkling surface. *La Baule Les Pins*, more than Kurys' other films, lends itself to analysis in terms of a heritage aesthetic whose nostalgic imagery of the past works to divert attention from a problematic present and cover over the subversive possibilities opened up by the narrative.[3] In *La Baule Les Pins*, Kurys' superbly lit reconstruction of daily life in a little family seaside town in the late 1950s (actually shot at the nearby beach of Le Pouliquen, since

3 For a discussion of the aesthetics of heritage cinema, see Andrew Higson (1993). See also my own article, Tarr (forthcoming).

the old town of La Baule Les Pins had been destroyed in the 1950s) provides a convincing, impressionistic backdrop of smells, colours, sounds and tastes. As Kurys claimed (1990), '[L]es années 50–60 ont une couleur, une atmosphère, une musique, une lumière particulière qui sont très cinématographiques'.[4] She wanted each prop to count, 'The pleasure consists in saying "Ah yes, we had this very can of Fly-Tox at home"; it's like eating a lot of Proustian madeleines' (Vincendeau 1991: 69). For example, the scene of Odette settling down in bed on her first night in the villa displays for the spectator the iron bedstead, Odette's night-dress and hair curlers, the trailing electric wires and the 1950s wireless, alarm clock and bedside lamp. Food plays a particularly evocative role in the film, be it through the ice lollies and cornets of peanuts that the children eat on the beach, the unsavoury-looking pasta and rice pudding which Odette serves up to the children at mealtimes, the mountain of sandwiches made for them by Michel, or the fresh sardines Léon purchases for the last family meal. The meticulous detail of the *mise-en-scène*, especially necessary for an intimate film shot in Cinemascope, can appear overwhelming, and was described by Daniel Toscan du Plantier (1990) as 'une évocation douloureuse, tant elle met de force et d'émotion'.[5] It invites nostalgia in particular when combined with panning camera movements, as in the shot near the beginning of Sophie in her winter socks and shoes, holding her doll, the first shots of the family on the beach, the children's sandcastle com-petition, and the extended family formed by the two households sitting round the table at their final supper together.

If the soundtrack functions primarily to establish period authenticity, the music, a mix of period and incidental music, functions additionally to underline moments of emotion. The sound of The Platters transports the spectator back to the 1950s, and the film's diegetic music includes 'Music from Paris' on Odette's wireless, 'Dream Lover' on Frédérique's transistor (just as Jean-Claude appears) and a waltz and a cha-cha played by the

---

4 '[T]he 1950s have a particular colour, atmosphere, sound and light, which is very cinematic'.

5 'painfully evocative, she puts so much force and emotion into it'.

nightclub band. The rather bland incidental piano and orchestral music, composed by Philippe Sarde, accompanies key stages in the drama, and evokes sympathy for all the participants, be it Sophie witnessing her parents not speaking, Frédérique recounting her feelings about Daniel, Léna meeting Jean-Claude on the beach, Michel looking at Léna before smashing up her car, the last family meal, or Léna telling Michel that it's all over. Sarde's sentimental song, 'La bouche pleine de sable',[6] written in the style of the period and sung by Julie Bataille/Frédérique, closes the film with blatantly nostalgic, if bitter-sweet memories of adolescence. However, nostalgia is also questioned through the scene in which Léna's night out with Jean-Claude, Bella and Léon is immortalised by a photograph taken of them dancing. The sepia-coloured image is completely at odds with the 'truth' of the situation. The photo portrays the couples dancing with each other's partners, Bella with Jean-Claude, Léna with Léon, and fails to register Léon's antagonism towards Jean-Claude and Léna's despair at being forced to choose between a life with Jean-Claude and her love for her children. The photo offers a note of warning to the spectator, even as it functions as a souvenir of the evening, highlighting the discrepancy between image and reality and pointing to the heartbreak which lies below the nostalgic surface.

In *Coup de foudre*, the *mise-en-scène* is integral to the development of the characters and the drama rather than being subsumed into the pleasures of visual spectacle. An analysis of *La Baule Les Pins*' treatment of fashion and cars will allow a comparison to be made between the two films. In *La Baule Les Pins*, there is, not unexpectedly, a similar devotion to the detail and authenticity of the 'look' of the characters (Richard Berry deliberately put on weight for his role), particularly their beachwear (allowing Léon to trick Odette into letting slip the top of her newly fashionable bikini). But Nathalie Baye's multiple changes of costume were perceived by some critics as simply reproductions of images from the fashion magazines of the day. Instead of representing female autonomy, female friendship and the rift between husband and

6 'A mouth full of sand.'

wife, as in *Coup de foudre*, fashion here carries a lesser weight of meaning. Nevertheless, it still serves to highlight ambivalent attitudes towards the mother: when Léna slips into a little black dress, one daughter objects to it being too tight while the other approves; and whereas Sophie plays at being grown-up by trying on her mother's makeup and high-heeled shoes, M. Ruffier focuses on the noise of Léna's high heels as a way of displaying his disapproval of her behaviour.

However, it is the period car which, in *La Baule Les Pins*, most contributes to characterisation and drama instead of merely inviting visual pleasure. Léon's way of careering all over the road when he is driving the family car (an Aronde) may delight the children but fails to amuse his wife, and his thoughtless machismo provokes a near collision with Jean-Claude and causes the death of the family cat. Cleaning the car provokes a symbolic quarrel between Léon and Daniel, his oldest son, whose autonomy Léon refuses to acknowledge. Different attitudes towards the car also crystallise the tension between Léon and Jean-Claude, who drives a powerful motorbike, sign of his youthfulness and freedom, and whose work as a sculptor takes the form of making art objects out of compressed cars. But most importantly, the car is the site of the power struggle between Léna and Michel. When Michel smashes Léna's newly purchased Renault Dauphine by driving, first the rear against a wall, then the front against a tree, he is smashing the visible sign of her new-found independence.[7] The heritage object, like the mirror in the later scene of his fight with Léna (and like the boutique in *Coup de foudre*), is quite literally destroyed. It is difficult for the spectator not to be aware of the underlying tensions which surface in such a dramatic moment and the violence of *La Baule Les Pins* may be all the more effective for taking place in such an otherwise picturesque context.

Kurys' first three films invite the spectator to read their family narratives against the background of the general upheavals in French society of the period. *La Baule Les Pins* is set at the time of

7 A similar analysis of the gendered use and abuse of cars is to be found in Christiane Rochefort's novels of the 1960s.

the Cold War, in the year in which de Gaulle was re-elected to power in order to restore order in Algeria, an election which brought the Fourth Republic to an end. However, references to political events are virtually evacuated in this film: Léon reads in the paper about trouble in Algeria caused by floods, a headline in *France Soir* refers to de Gaulle's speech to the Algerians, and M. Ruffier makes a reference to sputniks. But the film actually contains as many references to the war years as to current events: there is a bunker in the garden of the villa, Frédérique's voice-over informs the spectator that her grandparents died in the war, and Bella reveals that Michel saved both her and Léna from the deportation camp at Rivesaltes. These references remind the spectator of the characters' Jewish origins but the film does not pursue their ethnicity any further. Instead it focuses, as in *Coup de foudre*, on the modernisation taking place in 1950s France, with Michel promising to buy Odette a new Bendix washing machine, and on the influence of American culture, with the children having their first taste of Coca Cola (which they think is revolting). The fascination with America is also figured through the lure of New York for Jean-Claude, who has been offered a sculpture exhibition there. However, the absence of more polemical contemporary references makes *La Baule Les Pins* a more self-contained piece than Kurys' previous period films, justified, perhaps, by its summer holiday setting and focus on childhood.

At the same time, the film continues to explore the effects of a repressive patriarchal social structure which leads to women's desire for divorce and independence (though the breakdown between the parents is given from the beginning of the film), and to privilege the point of view of girls and women (though the women-centred focus of *Diabolo menthe* and *Coup de foudre* is attenuated here by the number of male characters). The representation of the two sisters, now aged somewhere between the ages of the sisters in the previous films, reproduces the feelings of helplessness and rebelliousness produced by their lack of comprehension of events over which they have no control and which will mark them for life. Frédérique only discovers what is really going on between her parents when Suzanne tells her what she has heard the grown-ups saying, and the two sisters instinctively react to their situation by being rude and difficult. Though they giggle together over the tricks they play on Odette and the landlord, share the horror of their parents' fighting and lament the loss of the stray dog, the film also explores their jealousies of one another and their different relationships with boys. While Sophie submits to playing doctors and nurses with René (she is more animated when playing a teacher), Frédérique falls in love with Daniel, gets him interested in her, and then falls out of love again, the story of her adolescent crush being told entirely from her point of view. Like *Diabolo menthe*, then, the film delicately sketches in a phase in their growing up. What the film lacks, though, is the range of girl characters of *Diabolo menthe* and the pleasure in girls' talk. Although *La Baule Les Pins* foregrounds the girls' point of view, it is also concerned with observing the children as a group, and is sympathetic to the way boys, too, are damaged by the incomprehensible and irrational behaviour of adults. René, the creative child who wins the sandcastle competition, still wets the bed, to his mother's amusement, while Daniel, who pretends to be older and more experienced than his years, has a strained relationship with his father, who mocks his son's academic aspirations and gets violently angry with him at the least provocation.

If the theme of friendship between girls, central to *Diabolo menthe*, gives way to relationships with boys in *La Baule Les Pins*, so the theme of friendship between women, central to *Coup de foudre*, is relegated to a less prominent place. That said, the representation of the friendship between Léna, the transgressive, independent woman, and Bella, her half-sister, mother of four and pregnant, is one of the major pleasures of the film. According to Bella, who describes their past history to Odette, the two women grew up together when her widowed father married Léna's widowed mother and were never parted until Léna got married. Michel is purported to have saved them both from the deportation camp, and Léon even suggests that Michel nearly married Bella instead. The closeness of their friendship, their complicity and tenderness, is demonstrated in the film through the use of two-shots of the two women sharing secrets. At the crazy-golf course, Léna tells Bella that she would leave immediately if it were not for the children; hanging out the washing with Bella, she confides how she had never known sexual pleasure until she slept with Jean-Claude. These moments share with *Coup de foudre* the notion that sexual pleasure with men takes on meaning through the relaying of the details to a female friend. But the relationship between Léna and Bella lacks the more explicitly voiced undercurrents of desire and the shared yearning for independence which united Léna and Madeleine in *Coup de foudre*.

In *La Baule Les Pins*, Léna functions primarily as an example of a woman who puts her own desires before those of the family. Kurys (1990) describes her as 'un personnage ambigu, on l'aime et on la déteste en même temps. Elle est celle qui fait souffrir.'[8] The film does not address the particular economic, cultural and affective reasons for the breakdown of Léna's marriage, as in *Coup de foudre*, but rather explores its effects. In the pre-credit sequence, the father is reduced to tears and the children abandoned on the train; at the end the father has to leave and the children have to adapt to his leaving. As Anne de Gasperi (1990) puts it, 'Elle part pour exister, vivre sa vie et en même temps casser tout derrière elle.'[9] Negative reactions to her behaviour are expressed through insert shots of the disapproving landlord and his family listening to the parents fighting, and through the gossiping of Bella and Odette. But, as Nathalie Baye points out, Léna's decision to leave her husband, not to be with another man but to live her own life and be free, makes her a woman ahead of her time (Pantel 1989). For Jill Forbes (1991: 68–9), the film succeeds in capturing the period when women were beginning to question financial security as a value and to seek satisfaction through claiming their sexual and professional independence. Léna is breaking the rules by leaving her husband, having a passionate sexual relationship with a younger lover, and wanting a divorce, a job, a car, a flat of

8 'an ambiguous character whom people love and hate at the same time. She makes others suffer.'

9 'She leaves in order to exist, to live her own life and at the same time to destroy everything behind her.'

her own, and custody of her daughters. Furthermore, despite her initial abandoning of them at the station, Léna is not actually demonised but portrayed as a loving mother too.[10] She gives her daughters physical affection, tries (eventually) to explain to them what has happened to her relationship with their father, and comforts them after the quarrel with Michel. Although for some critics, Baye hides her feelings so well that the spectator does not know what is going on (Tranchant 1989), arguably Baye's performance is nuanced and convincing as the mother who loves her children but wants to lead her own life and fantasises momentarily about running away to America with her dream lover. In this film, then, the mother is more sympathetic than the authoritarian mother of *Diabolo menthe*. Nevertheless, the cut from Sophie crying 'je veux ma maman'[11] to a shot of the monstrous boar's head, complete with fangs, on the living-room wall of the rented villa, perhaps unintentionally signals a more ambivalent attitude.

The other women in the film, both mothers, contrast significantly with Léna. Bella's placidity and willingness to compromise underline Léna's courage and daring while Odette's status indicates how privileged she is. The pregnant Bella is fascinated by Léna's exploits, supports her decisions (except when they disagree as to which child has won at Lotto), and shares complicit looks with her when the men do something particularly stupid; but there is no question of her having the courage (or the desire) to take a similar course of action. Her life is fully invested in her husband and children and she spends her spare time knitting for the (fifth) baby to be. Yet her fascination with Léna, her visible impatience with her husband and her lack of desire for sex hints that such a life is not entirely fulfilling. Her unplanned pregnancy raises both the practical question of the need for birth control (contraception was not legally available in the 1950s) and the more ideological question of the validity and desirability of maternity as woman's destiny. Odette, on the other hand, provides an example

10 Forbes compares Baye's role here with her role as an aberrant mother in Nicole Garcia's *Un weekend sur deux* (1990), where she is less sexually active and more heavily censured by her children.

11 'I want my mummy.'

of a working-class woman and single parent who needs to earn a living to support her children and is therefore obliged to leave her two boys with their grandmother while she does so. She responds vehemently to the landlord's intrusive questioning by denying the existence of a father, 'il n'y a pas de père – il n'y a jamais eu',[12] although the motive for this denial is left for the spectator to guess at. Nevertheless, the film pursues the theme of women's assumption of responsibility for their children and preference for not being dependent on men across class barriers, confirming the critique of marriage and the couple already proffered in *Coup de foudre*.

The unsatisfactory nature of marriage is primarily figured through the representation of the husbands who, as in *Coup de foudre*, are treated with a certain amount of sympathy at the same time as they are shown to be unable to measure up to female desire. Richard Berry physically changed for the role of Michel, putting on weight and shaving his hair to appear more middle aged and unattractive. A man who loves his wife and children without having any understanding of why the marriage is no longer working, Michel reacts to his situation first with tears, then by staying away. He only appears at the holiday villa two-thirds of the way through the film, bearing gifts which include, significantly, a camera for Frédérique. He then reacts to the discovery that Léna has been having an affair by attempting emotional blackmail and scaring the children about being sent away to school. It is evident that he does not really know how to communicate with them (he gets Frédérique's age wrong) or look after them (the awkward restaurant scene recalls a parallel scene in *Diabolo menthe*). Léna's appearance provokes him to insults (he calls her a prostitute as opposed to a dyke, as in *Coup de foudre*) and unacceptable violence, yet he still hopes they can start again. His desolation, isolation and lack of comprehension make him sympathetic, like the stray dog which attaches itself to him when he arrives at La Baule and has to be chained to the roadside at the end. But his jealousy and possessiveness, his fixation on his role

12 'there's no father, there never was'.

as breadwinner, his failure to understand his wife's need for independence, and his inability to communicate except when driven to physical violence mean that there is no possibility of compromise.

Jean-Pierre Bacri, who played Costa in *Coup de foudre*, plays Léon as a character who combines Michel's physical affection for children with Costa's childlike inadequacies. Léon is first seen emerging from the sea where he has been playing with the children, wearing seaweed like a wig, a good-humoured, loveable clown who amuses the children and at the end offers Frédérique a shoulder to cry on if she misses her father. Léon shows solidarity with Michel, though he also reproaches him for spending too much time at work and not enough with his family. But he is often a trial to Bella (he cannot sleep at night without complete darkness and no noise, for example) and his occasionally petulant, authoritarian behaviour can be attributed to feelings of inadequacy which derive from his lack of education. Although he is less jinxed than Costa, he drives dangerously, treats his oldest son belligerently, and gets lumbered with fifty kilos of fresh sardines just in order to get a good price from the local fisherman! The camera's focus on Bella's weary but tolerant reactions produces a critique of his behaviour, as does the quarrel he provokes with Jean-Claude which reveals his ignorance and prejudices.

The husbands of *La Baule Les Pins* are as inadequate as the husbands of *Coup de foudre*, but *La Baule Les Pins* also offers a contrasting representation of a 'dream lover'. Jean-Claude, played by Vincent Lindon (who had the thankless role of what Kurys calls the 'mec–copain–amant–frère qu'on quitte pour une passion'[13] in *Un homme amoureux*), is an artist, like Madeleine in *Coup de foudre*, and shares her passion and enthusiasm. A successful young sculptor, whom Léna met at an exhibition in Lyons, he has an exhibition opening in New York, where he intends to stay. First sighted as a well-endowed body on the beach, he proves to be a sexy, passionate lover. He is also a romantic figure, a man in love who wants Léna to marry him and go away with him, leaving

13 'bloke–friend–lover–brother that you leave for a passionate affair'.

everything behind her.[14] His motorbike, leather gear and tent are signs of his mobility and freedom, his art form a rejection of the modern consumer-driven world. In the end, though, Jean-Claude shocks Léna by failing to wait for her at their last rendezvous, which she misses because of the children going missing. His departure means that Léna does not actually have to choose between her lover and her daughters. But it is also a sign that the most desirable of men is still insensitive to the everyday realities of women's lives.

Because of its focus on childhood and summer holidays, *La Baule Les Pins* may appear at first sight as a rather slight film. As a contribution to the 'summer-holiday movie' genre, it is far removed from the slapstick antics of Jacques Tati in *Monsieur Hulot's Holiday* (Jacques Tati, 1953), actually shot on the same beach. It also marginalises the normal focus on the romantic misadventures of teenagers and young adults, like Cliff Richard's *Summer Holiday* (Peter Yates, 1963) or Eric Rohmer's *Pauline à la plage* (1983). Rather, Kurys seeks to recapture an authenticity of period to explore the experiences of childhood, in line with the work of the filmmakers she most admires, like François Truffaut's *Les 400 coups* (1959), Federico Fellini's *Amarcord* (1974) and Ingmar Bergman's *Fanny and Alexander* (1982). Kurys invests those experiences with a mature analysis of factors contributing to the difficulties of interpersonal and intergenerational relationships in the 1950s. Though she dilutes the female-centred perspectives of her earlier films, preferring 'une légèreté à la Trenet'[15] (Neuhoff 1990), the sparkling images of the past are informed by a sophisticated awareness of the troubled relationships between adults and how adult behaviour can affect children's lives. Yet it is still possible for spectators to concentrate only on the film's surface pleasures, as is clear from Pierre Vavasseur's summing up of the film's qualities (1992), intended as a tribute, '*La Baule Les Pins* est l'exemple même de la comédie de mœurs française:

---

14 Kurys felt that Jean-Claude resembled a Jean Marais character from the 1950s, like the eponymous hero of Jean Cocteau's *Orphée* (1950), perhaps.
15 'a Trenet-style lightness of touch.'

un zeste d'autobiographie, un soupçon d'enfance, un peu d'humour, un peu d'amertume et beaucoup de tendresse en filigrane'.[16]

References

Forbes, Jill (1991), '*La Baule-Les Pins (C'est la vie)*', *Monthly Film Bulletin*, 58: 686.

Gasperi, Anne de (1990), '*La Baule, Les Pins*', *Le Quotidien de Paris*, 17 and 18 February.

Higson, Andrew (1993), 'Re-presenting the National Past: Nostalgia and Pastiche in the Heritage Film', in Lester Friedman (ed.), *British Cinema and Thatcherism: Fires Were Started*, London, UCL Press, 109–29.

Kurys, Diane (1990), 'Entretien avec Diane Kurys', *La Baule Les Pins*, publicity brochure.

Neuhoff, Eric (1990), '*La Baule Les Pins* de Diane Kurys, la fin de l'été', *Madame Figaro*, 3 February.

Pantel, Monique (1989), 'Six enfants volent la vedette à Nathalie Baye', *France Soir*, 28 September.

Tarr, Carrie, 'Heritage, nostalgia and the woman's film: the case of Diane Kurys' in Sue Harris and Elizabeth Ezra (eds), *Visual Culture and French National Identity* (forthcoming).

Toscan du Plantier, Daniel (1990), 'La douleur faite à l'enfance', *Le Figaro Magazine*, 19 February.

Tranchant, Marie-Noëlle (1989), 'Diane Kurys: une odeur d'ambre solaire', *Le Figaro*, 22 August.

Vavasseur, Pierre (1992), '*La Baule Les Pins* sur Antenne 2', *Le Parisien*, 5 May.

Vincendeau, Ginette (1991), 'Like eating a lot of madeleines', *Monthly Film Bulletin*, 58: 686, 69–70.

---

16 '*La Baule Les Pins* is a perfect example of the French comedy of manners: a dash of autobiography, a soupçon of childhood, a touch of humour, a little bitterness and lots of underlying tenderness.'

6

Après l'amour

After *La Baule Les Pins*, Kurys felt the need to leave family and childhood memories behind and work once again on a film with a contemporary setting. *Après l'amour*, co-written with Antoine Lacomblez, was triggered by observations of life around her in the early 1990s, specifically the apparently arbitrary break-ups of relationships in her circle of friends and acquaintances. She wanted the film to provide a portrait of the generation which, twenty years earlier, had broken with conventional morality and tried to find another way of loving. So the complicated love lives of *Après l'amour*'s well-heeled thirty-something Parisian professionals reflect what Danièle Heymann called, the 'blues de la pré-quarantaine, la mélancholie brouillonne des adolescents de mai 68 qui crurent pouvoir larguer les amarres'[1] (Heymann 1992). As Kurys explained in an interview published in the film's publicity brochure (Kurys 1992), she was concerned with exploring the reasons for people staying together or leaving one another, the possibility of someone loving two people at once and the feasibility of allowing the person one loves the freedom to explore other desires. Unlike the typical French comedy of manners, *Après l'amour* refuses to take the traditional couple for granted as either the starting point or the end point of the narrative.

While the range of characters, though limited, enables the film to provide a study of contemporary social mores, *Après l'amour*'s

1 'pre-forties blues, the confused melancholy of people who were adolescents in May 68 and thought they could go their own way'.

central female character, Lola, 'the modern woman', is clearly modelled on Kurys herself:

> Lola, c'est moi. J'ai essayé d'être le plus sincère possible. Et puis c'est quelqu'un d'autre parce qu'elle est jouée par Isabelle Huppert. C'est le symbole de la 'femme moderne'. Indépendante. Elle gagne son argent. Elle décide de sa vie. Elle ne subit pas. C'est une femme libre qui ne se raconte pas d'histoires. Qui ne mélange pas tout. Alors bien sûr, elle peut être vue comme quelqu'un de froid et d'égoïste[2] (Kurys 1992).

In fact, despite the evacuation of references to Kurys' childhood family situation (the first of her films to do so), a number of factors suggest that *Après l'amour* is just as personal as her earlier films, if not more so. Isabelle Huppert had become a close friend of Kurys since *Coup de foudre* and, cast in the role of Lola, she functions as Kurys' *alter ego*, 'Je me disais toujours que, si jamais je faisais un film où je me projetais moi, à mon âge, je la prendrais, elle. Il y a une adéquation entre elle et moi'[3] (Kurys 1992). Huppert's presence invites comparisons to be made between Lola, the 'modern woman', and Léna, the mother struggling for independence whom she played in *Coup de foudre*. Her ability to recall the mother figure as she plays the daughter becomes even more significant when it transpires that Lola is pregnant, a theme inspired by Kurys' own pregnancy during the shooting of *La Baule Les Pins*. The themes of the couple at risk from the complication of a triangular situation and the jealousy of the lover's wife are reprised from *Un Homme amoureux*. And Lola's role as a successful writer provides a follow-up to Jane's role in *Un Homme amoureux* and invites the spectator to read her questioning of the relationship between her life and her work as a

---

2 'Lola is me. I've tried to be as sincere as possible. But she's also someone else because she's played by Isabelle Huppert. She's the symbol of "the modern women". Independent. She earns her money. She makes her own decisions. She doesn't submit to things. She's a free woman with no illusions. Who doesn't muddle everything up. So, of course, she can be seen as a rather cold, selfish person.'

3 'I always said that, if ever I made a film in which I projected myself at my age, I'd cast her. We match each other.'

reflection of Kurys' own doubts and beliefs about her work as a filmmaker.

Après l'amour focuses on the central character of Lola, an unmarried novelist with no children and no apparent desire for children. Lola lives with her long-term lover David (Bernard Giraudeau), an architect, and is having an affair with Tom (Hippolyte Girardot), a rock musician. But David and Tom are both devoted fathers and unable (or unwilling) to break off their relationship with the mothers of their children, David with Marianne (Lio), Tom with Elisabeth (Laure Killing), in order to commit themselves fully to Lola. The unsatisfactory nature of their relationships affects Lola's writing and David's interactions at work, especially with his assistant Rachel (Judith Reval) and his half-brother Romain (Yvan Attal), who in turn has an unsatisfactory relationship with Anne (Ingrid Held). The film explores the consequences of the breakdown of traditional assumptions about the couple and gender roles through Lola's ambivalent attitudes towards men and motherhood, and David, Tom and Romain's ambivalent attitudes towards women and fatherhood.

The narrative structure of *Après l'amour* is articulated through a year in the life of Lola and David, beginning and ending with David's party for Lola's birthday, complete with cake, candles and champagne. In the opening sequence, Lola absents herself for a brief but blissful embrace with Tom; and in the closing sequence, she absents herself with David, leaving her guests once more to blow out the candles. The cyclical plot is typical of Kurys' films, but there is also a linear development in that, at the end of the film, Lola has stopped seeing Tom and is expecting David's baby. The fragility of the open couple Lola forms with David is highlighted through two narrative strands: Lola's clandestine, fragmented and unsatisfactory affair with Tom, and David's tempestuous relationship with the dramatic and unpredictable Marianne. Lola's passionate and not so passionate encounters with Tom are brought to an end when Elisabeth interrupts their stay in Pompeii, and Lola discovers that Tom is really committed to his (possibly adulterous) wife. But David's involvement with Marianne leads, first, to him agreeing to take the children away when she gets hysterical about his lack of commitment and then, after her attempted suicide, agreeing to move in with her again. At this point, Lola invites David to move out permanently and sets about living on her own. She confides to Romain, on his wedding day, that she is pregnant, starts work on her new novel and subsequently resumes her relationship with David (who is now living with Marianne). When she finally tells David she is pregnant, he responds with a question, 'Qu'est-ce que je vais faire à Noël, moi?.'[4] The narrative structure may (or may not) point to a positive development for Lola, but David will now have to negotiate between his two families at Christmas as well as between his two women during the rest of the year. So the problematic network of relationships and commitments remains.

The ambivalence of the ending is matched by the disconcerting ups and downs of the film's episodic structure. The lack of plot means that, typically of a Kurys film, each episode has to be appreciated in and of itself, for the accuracy of its observation and the way it builds up the characters and their relationships. For Kurys, the scene in which Elisabeth gets hysterical over a travel bag because she suspects, rightly, that Tom is having an affair, manages to convey all one needs to know about the character, 'Il suffit de voir une femme piquer une crise ne nerfs à cause d'un sac de voyage pour savoir qui elle est, comment elle va, comment elle aime … C'est le détail qui tue'[5] (Kurys 1992). For Jean-Claude Philippe (1992), the scene where Tom drags an unsuspecting Lola out to help him surprise his wife with her (supposed) lover is so preposterous that it must have been based on an actual event. But the spectator's pleasure in the narrative is marred by the film's indecision as to whether or not it is centred on Lola and by the lack of agency afforded the central characters. Lola's voice-over and the scenes of Lola at work on her writing punctuate the narrative and so foreground her role, since no other character is afforded this form or degree of subjectivity. But the film cuts between characters rather than fully privileging Lola's point of view and her presence

4 'What am I going to do at Christmas?'
5 'All you need is to see a woman getting hysterical about a travel bag to know who she is, what state she's in, how she loves … It's the detail which is devastating.'

as the subject of the narrative is curiously ambivalent and muted. Furthermore, David and Lola both seem to submit to events rather than control them. David takes at face value whatever proposal is made to him, letting himself be seduced by Rachel, emotionally blackmailed by Marianne and asked to leave by Lola. Lola too, despite her active decision to have an affair with Tom and, later, to let David go, is reacting to situations created by others. She stays out of David's relationship with Marianne and waits passively for Tom to take the initiative in his affair with her. Even her pregnancy comes as a surprise (the lovemaking scene between David and Lola starts off as a quarrel), and the absence of debate about the desirability of her having a child suggests that she is letting nature take its course rather than deciding for herself. Her passivity and solitude are underlined by various shots of her lying alone in bed after her lover's departure. The uncertainties and impasses of the narrative, then, reflect the impossibility, or at least the difficulty, of both sustaining the couple and exercising control over one's life.

The characters' emotional crises are offered up to the spectator within settings which display the affluent lifestyles of the professional middle classes. Lola and David's duplex is elegantly designed and lit and full of paintings and sculptures; Marianne lives in a spacious flat with long if lugubrious corridors; Tom has a magnificent villa outside Paris; Romain's wedding reception is held in a riverside house with a huge, tropical conservatory. As in *Un Homme amoureux*, the city of Paris itself is constructed through recognisable tourist shots: when Tom and Lola meet at the Hilton, the film cuts to shots of the Arc de Triomphe and the Eiffel Tower by night; and when Rachel seduces David, the empty flat on the Ile St Louis is illuminated by the lights of the passing *bateaux-mouches*. The characters do not interact with others outside their social circle, even in the film's more ordinary settings like the train, the supermarket or the Japanese restaurant. The Jewishness of the central characters is played down, there are no working-class characters, and a brief glimpse of a black face or two at Lola's birthday parties is the only concession to a contemporary multi-ethnic France, just as the empty factory, which David is due to convert into offices, is the only setting which calls attention to France's declining postindustrial economic situation. The film's music also fails to capture a sense of contemporaneity, particularly problematic in a film which centres, unconvincingly, on a leather-jacketed rock musician as one of its central characters. Tom's guitar composition for Lola is anaemic, his studio recording session lacks energy and the group of rockers hired for Romain and Anne's 'white' wedding sing American fifties hits in bad English. Yves Simon's incidental music is rather like Tom's, professional but lifeless, failing to underpin the film with any real feeling. The *mise-en-scène* and soundtrack of *Après l'amour*, then, fail to do what Kurys' period films do, that is, capture the complex realities of a changing French society. Instead they offer up a hermetically-sealed, privileged social world which may not be recognisable to the majority of contemporary French cinema-goers.

On a formal level, however, *Après l'amour* shows evidence of research into the aesthetic possibilities of the image. The subtle, stylised use of colour and lighting produces effects which undermine the surface complacency of sounds and settings. From the pre-credit sequence onwards, the screen is suffused with a *gamme* of yellows, browns and greys. Despite the occasional red flourish, like the scarf worn by Lola at the recording studio and the red suit Marianne wears to go out with David, the image track is dominated by this limited colour range which works to consolidate a jaundiced view of the characters' feelings and relationships. Furthermore, a significant number of scenes take place at night in the dark, especially the sex scenes, which tend also to be set in confining and uncomfortable places. Lola first kisses Tom in his car as the rain lashes down around them; Tom takes her off for the night to a grotty room in the Eden Hotel [*sic*] on the main road outside Tourcoing; Lola persuades Tom to stay behind overnight in the ruins at Pompeii; David makes love to Marianne in the doorway to an apartment block. The obscurity of these scenes produces, literally, a dark view of the sexual relationships involved, and contrasts with the only (procreative) sex scene between the main couple, which takes place in the day in their brightly lit shower. The darkness extends to the workplace, too, Tom's studio and David's office being shot in heavy shadow (in contrast to the bleached out light used in the shots of Lola's studio, discussed below). Light brought to the scene only tends to reveal deception, as when the candle-lit cake is brought in at Lola's birthday parties. The switching on of Lola's bedroom light highlights David's duplicitous behaviour; the switching on and off of the children's bedroom light at Marianne's flat signals David and Marianne's bad faith; the light from the *bateaux-mouches* illuminates David's infidelity with Rachel; the play of lights in the hotel rooms in Italy reveals Elisabeth and Lola's presence to each other; and Elisabeth's infidelity to Tom is signalled by a light in her lover's apartment block. The corresponding lack of illumination in the characters' relationships (or their lack of desire to illuminate their relationships) is further signalled by the ways in which they turn away from each other, refuse to reply directly to questions, are often unable to look the other in the eye, and cannot express their commitment. This is particularly true of the last exchange between Lola and David, which is both humorous and moving in its demonstration of the continuing difficulty they experience in expressing their feelings about one another, even as a result of Lola's pregnancy. Their deceptive looks, gestures and words, like the deceptive lighting, leave the spectator to interpret what is going on beneath the surface or, as they disappear from the screen, in the dark.

The recurrent scenes set in Lola's airy and brightly lit penthouse study with its panoramic views over Paris (contrasting with the opaque glass wall which boxes in the characters in the flat below) are set up by the soundtrack and *mise-en-scène* as privileged moments within the film. These scenes, which foreground Lola as a successful career woman, provide an insight into the way in which her life and work are interconnected. The film initially draws attention to Lola's writer's block, brought about by the impasse in her relationships with her two lovers, through insert close-ups of the act of writing and crumpled pages in the waste-paper basket. Lola is trying, like Kurys, to find a way of using her experiences of life not as a diary but as the basis for fiction. Her problem lies in finding the inspiration to mediate her experiences, 'il faudrait que j'invente ma vie au lieu de la raconter'.[6] Her strategies for getting on with the task, like stopping herself writing every time she finds herself telling the truth, or writing in pencil instead of ink, are of no avail. She finds herself daydreaming instead, her black-and-white fantasies projected onto the screen formed by her penthouse window (the obsession with her inner life blocking her view of the wider world beyond the flat). In the first daydream, she goes to meet Tom at the airport, hides from him, and is then identified and embraced by him (a reworking of a scene in *Un homme amoureux*). In the second, after David has advised her to imagine the worst that could happen to them, she imagines a conversation in which David tells her that their relationship is over and he is leaving. Unable to do anything about either her writing or her relationships, she redecorates her study instead, clearing away the clutter (a nostalgic insert pans over treasured objects dating back to the writing of her first book) and making the room bright and white. In the penultimate sequence of the film, set in her study in the flat where she now lives on her own, her voice-over reveals that she has resumed writing (and is contemplating a chapter based on Romain and Anne's honeymoon in Ibiza), David is once more being allowed to comment on her drafts (which she had hidden from him during her affair with Tom), and she is working not just to the publisher's deadline, but (unknown to David) to a deadline determined by her pregnancy. The image shows her feverishly at work, her hair now done up in a pony tail. Her new situation has enabled her to overcome her writer's block and find inspiration.

Whilst the film charts Lola's difficulties in writing, it also stresses that she has already written three novels by the age of thirty-five (Kurys herself was thirty-eight when she made her fourth film). Her successful career and lack of a family allow her to be a free agent, but success alone does not bring her happiness. When Rachel suggests that her writing is a sign of self-love, Lola argues that self-portraits are not necessarily narcissistic but may

6 'I need to invent my life instead of recounting it'.

represent a need for others to identify with one's predicament and make one feel less alone in the world. However, when Olivier and Simon, David's children, ask her 'who she writes to', she replies 'no-one', then hastily amends her answer to 'everyone'. The uncertainty about whether or not her work is aimed at others is symptomatic of Lola's solipsism. Although she discusses her work with David, she is unwilling to enter into a dialogue about her books with her women readers, Rachel and Marianne, just as Kurys has been reluctant to enter into a dialogue with the women who enjoy her films. For Lola, art functions as a source of identity and a form of self-expression rather than as a means of communication. In *Après l'amour*, Lola's bland writing, like her inexpressive speech, does not communicate the 'truth' about her inner feelings, be it towards David or towards her pregnancy, but functions rather as an aesthetic device to affirm her self-image as a successful artist and, therefore (the film implies), a superior character.

The interest of *Après l'amour* lies in how Kurys' privileged 'modern woman' handles the tensions produced by her complicated relationships. But the film is further complicated by its ambivalent attitude towards women and, like *Cocktail Molotov*, lacks the examples of female intimacy to be found in Kurys' other films. *Après l'amour* sets up two types of women, 'lolas' and 'mariannes', cold independent women and hysterical dependent women, based on Kurys' thesis, expressed in the film's publicity brochure, that all women play both roles at various times in their lives. Not surprisingly, then, the film's attitude towards Lola's independence is as ambivalent as its construction of her open relationship with David. For Kurys, Lola's situation is typical, 'il y a beaucoup de filles comme ça, pas vraiment féministes, qui ont tout voulu à la fois ou qui n'ont pas su ce qu'elles voulaient. Elles se retrouvent un peu seules, un peu perdues'[7] (Kurys 1992). The film establishes Lola as a detached and superior woman by virtue of her situation as a professional writer, her childlessness and her ability to conduct her affairs just like a man, 'Lola, on la voit à

7 'there are a lot of women like that, not really feminists, who wanted to have it all or didn't know what they wanted. Now they're a bit lonely, a bit lost'.

peine se maquiller, s'habiller, faire la cuisine. Elle déteste les bijoux mais elle prend l'avion, repeint la maison, conduit, tape à la machine. Pas de crises d'hystérie'[8] (Kurys 1992). On the other hand, she wears clothes which are similar to those worn by the other more 'feminine' (and hysterical) women, be it a red scarf (like Rachel), a little black or white dress (like Anne), cream pyjamas (like Elisabeth) or a Japanese dressing-gown (like Marianne). Such similarities suggest that *Après l'amour* is working through unspoken fears that the differences between Lola and other women are less obvious than might otherwise be assumed. Lola's ambivalent attitudes towards other women, her lovers and, especially, motherhood can be attributed, then, to a crisis in her identity as a modern, independent woman.

Lola's comparative serenity and self-sufficiency are contrasted with the hysterical, manipulative behaviour of the women who are set up as her rivals. Taking the role of Susan in *Un homme amoureux* to an extreme, Marianne and Elisabeth are passionate, jealous women who are completely dependent on their male partners. Marianne has no visible form of paid employment and behaves in a duplicitous manner to wrest David away from Lola, pretending her son is ill, threatening to kill herself, making scenes in public, getting hysterical over her sons' absence and attempting suicide. Elisabeth is first seen assisting Tom in his work at the recording studio, but she gets hysterical when Tom borrows her travel bag without telling her, flies to Italy with the children to check up on him, and leaves evidence of an affair lying around in order (successfully) to make him jealous. Both these mothers are willing to put their children at risk to secure their man. Their behaviour contrasts negatively with the calm, unruffled way in which Lola interacts with David and Tom and looks after Simon and Olivier, the latter of whom rewards her with the gift of a drawing (a man falling into the water between two crocodiles). But Marianne and Elisabeth's hysterical complaints about their men's

---

8 'You hardly see Lola use makeup, get dressed, or do the cooking. She hates jewellery but she takes a plane, does the decorating, drives and types. Without any hysterical crises.'

shortcomings are actually quite accurate – David treats Marianne badly, Tom is having an affair – and Lola's refusal to make demands on her lovers, and her acceptance of their lack of commitment towards her, are ways of evading, rather than confronting this issue.

The problematic construction of other women applies also to the two younger women characters in the film. Anne is childlike, sexy and not very bright, factors which account for Romain's desire to marry her, and Rachel is a manipulative and vengeful nymphomaniac, who seduces David, attempts to seduce Romain, uses what she knows about David to try to poison his relationship with Lola and deliberately messes up David's contract for the design of the disused factory space. In contrast, Lola appears as the epitome of maturity, intelligence and sensitivity. But it is notable that Rachel calls into question Lola's difference from other women when she suggests that Lola's apparent acceptance of David's relationship with Marianne is actually just a strategy to keep him. Running through the film, then, is the disturbing thesis that the behaviour of the most liberated of women is actually motivated by the fear of losing her man. Not only does the film call into question the possibility of female autonomy, it allows Lola no independent women friends, colleagues, relatives or acquaintances, and so refuses to explore solidarity with other women as an alternative source of pleasure and fulfilment.

If a relationship with a man is the *sine qua non* of women's lives, the ways in which men are represented is of crucial significance. Yet *Après l'amour* does little more than rework the male characters familiar from Kurys' earlier films, making them just a little older and giving them parental responsibilities. Lola's closest relationships are with men rather than women: David, the soulmate she has known since the age of fifteen, and Romain, the friend she confides in, constitute her 'family' (like the young male duo of *Cocktail Molotov* for Anne), while Tom is her latest passion (recreating the triangular set-up of *Un Homme amoureux* centred on Jane). The three men, despite superficial differences, all share certain key characteristics: they are utterly charming and utterly unreliable. According to Kurys (1992), 'Tous les hommes sont des lâches attendrissants'.[9] What makes them attractive is their vulnerability, their ability to be supportive and caring, and their sensitivity as lovers. But on the negative side, they are unable to make an emotional commitment. The film acknowledges the tension generated by these two aspects of their characters without ever suggesting that their behaviour is unacceptable or that change is possible.

The men's vulnerability is signalled by their inability to understand what is going on around them. Romain and David are unaware of Rachel's scheming, and David does not see how he is being manipulated by Marianne, nor Tom by Elisabeth. This lack of awareness leaves them looking bewildered and helpless in the face of events: numerous shots show David unable to interpret what is happening to him, while Tom is frightened and pathetic when faced with his wife's infidelity (his childlike qualities having already been signalled in his birthday gift to Lola of a squeaky toy). Even Marianne's male babysitter is vulnerable, too frightened by Marianne's diatribe to ask for his money and then forced to grovel on the floor to pick it up. Male tenderness is shown through David and Tom's roles as affectionate, if absent, fathers, particularly through the motif of the father looking in on his children asleep in bed (like Michel in *Coup de foudre*). But the film recognises that the man is likely to opt out of actual childcare, since David gets Rachel to take Olivier and Simon to school for him, and Lola spends more time looking after them than David does. And although both David and Tom undertake certain domestic responsibilities – the opening and closing sequences start with David's hands in the sink preparing for Lola's party and Tom is seen doing the supermarket shopping for Elisabeth – their domestic roles are, nevertheless, fairly limited in scope.

Despite Marianne's denial of the importance of sex in her relationship with David, both David and Tom are represented as lovers able to give women pleasure. But the explicit sex scenes are problematic in that, even more than in *Un Homme amoureux*, they are filmed in a conventional manner which denies the female

9 'All men are disarming cowards.'

point of view and offers up the woman's fragmented body for the spectator's voyeuristic gaze. There are unnecessary fetichising close-ups of women's bare buttocks in the scenes when Tom and, later, David slip off Lola's panties and, again, in David's sex scene with Marianne; and in one of Lola's love scenes with Tom, a prosaic shot of him undoing her bra cuts to an unmotivated close-up of her left breast cupped by Tom's hand, a point of view available only to the voyeuristic camera/spectator, before cutting to Tom's face in medium close-up. Kurys may also be trying to emphasise the importance of women's sexual pleasure, as when Lola listens with pleasurable anticipation to Tom's fantasy over the telephone about their next meeting, or when David pursues her into the shower. However, the scenes where women take the sexual initiative (Lola in the ruins of Pompeii, Rachel in her seduction of David) are followed by scenes of retribution (Lola's loss of Tom, Rachel's loss of David's sympathy), and the sexually active Lola is repeatedly, if temporarily, left lying alone in bed, abandoned by her lover. *Après l'amour* thus betrays a lingering uneasiness with women's sexuality and the notion of women as the sexual equals of men.

The men's failure to stay with Lola is symptomatic of their chronic infidelity, lack of responsibility and lack of commitment. As Claude Gonzalez phrased it, the men are 'lâches, menteurs, inconséquents, irresponsables même, nuls' as well as being 'incapables d'exprimer, de savoir ce qu'ils veulent, écartelés, mufles ou puérils, faibles'[10] (Gonzalez 1992) . David is seduced by Rachel, Romain is ready to succumb to Rachel's advances on his wedding day, Tom refuses to acknowledge that his infidelity is of the same order as Elisabeth's. Furthermore, they are unable to communicate their emotions honestly: Tom walks out on Lola and Elisabeth rather than discuss his or their feelings; David avoids talking directly to Lola and Marianne about the things that matter (he does not even know which of his 'wives' to expect at the hospital after Marianne's suicide attempt); the rupture of David's

10 'Cowards, liars, frivolous, irresponsible, useless' ... 'incapable of expressing themselves or of knowing what they want, tormented, boorish or puerile, and weak.'

relationship with Lola is brought about when he begins to shout at her as he shouts at the people at work. Although these men are successful professionally, they are unable to manage their relationships with women and at the end of the film, despite the assumed reformation of the David/Lola couple, the future is still uncertain. Indeed, the most affectionate relationship depicted in the film is that between David and Romain who, despite their quarrel, share a level of physical intimacy and verbal banter which is lacking in the relationships between men and women. Though the film assumes the desirability of the heterosexual couple, then, it also recognises that reality falls well short of the ideal.

What, then, is the role of motherhood is this unsatisfactory situation? At the beginning of the film Lola attributes the difficulties in her relationships with David and Tom to the existence of their children and concludes, 'il faudrait pas faire d'enfants'.[11] She tells Tom that she has never wanted a child and points out that many women have children for the wrong reasons, like wanting company or trying to cling on to 'une histoire d'amour'. Tom looks incredulous and argues that it is better to risk having a child than regret not having done it. The close-up of his interrogatory look invites the spectator to share his view. Yet the film's overall attitude towards the desirability of motherhood remains thoroughly ambivalent. Lola's distrust of motherhood is confirmed by Marianne's and Elisabeth's abject behaviour as mothers and the children's roles as either helpless witnesses of their parents' quarrels or instruments of emotional blackmail (like the young girls of *Coup de foudre* and *La Baule Les Pins*). The film's only reference to its title also implies that what comes after love is a form of punishment. During their visit of the frescoes at Pompeii, Tom explains how retribution was visited upon those whose loss of faith had led to decadence, 'après l'amour ils ont été punis'.[12] The collapse of meaning between notions of love and decadence links Pompeii to the permissive sixties (and the 'Love' emblazoned on the Citroën DS of *Cocktail Molotov*) and suggests

11 'one shouldn't have children.'
12 'after love, they were punished'.

that happiness in the modern world has been compromised by the loss of faith in traditional moral values and the decadence of multiple sexual liaisons and parenting outside marriage. However, Lola herself comes to contest this logic, just as she had contested Tom's reading of the Pompeii frescoes by expressing a desire to make love with a satyr. At the end of the film, her pregnancy has not (yet) made her resemble Marianne and Elisabeth or reduced her relationship with David to one of dependency. Instead, it has given her life a new focus, enabled her to progress with her book and made her the centre of attention of friends who approve of her condition.

However, the film's elliptical narrative structure means that the spectator is not invited to share in the process by which Lola decides to keep the baby. Her motivation is therefore open to speculation. Has she simply responded to Tom's advice to take action rather than risk regretting not having done so? Is she deploying a tactic to sustain her relationship with David? Has her experience of looking after David's children shown her that she is capable of relating to children? Is having a child another form of narcissistic solipsism, like her writing? Or is the film suggesting that a woman really is only fulfilled through having a baby? And if so, will Lola be forced to give up her writing and eventually turn into another Marianne? Or will her inner strength, writing talent and economic independence enable her to transcend the predicaments of more ordinary women? Huppert's understated, low-key performance as Lola provides few clues, but her last words affirm that looking for a name for the baby is like looking for the first words of a new novel. If the film has an optimistic ending, it is that a new novel, a new story, is possible, and that the female writer will be able to allay her fears about what motherhood does to women and combine motherhood and creativity. But on the negative side, the fact that Lola's pregnancy provides copy for her writing, and the absence of any visualisation of her as an actual mother (she even turns away from David's sons at Romain's wedding), mean that her pregnancy functions primarily as an abstract idea, an aesthetic device which provides a satisfactory ending for what would otherwise be a repetitive, cyclical drama.

Après l'amour is a less adventurous film than Kurys' other movies to date in that its subject matter, affairs of the heart in a carefully depicted middle-class setting, is the stuff of French art cinema, but is not inflected by a focus on the interests and desires of a plurality of women. The film invites comparison with the work of Claude Sautet, whose intimist middle-class dramas like *Les Choses de la vie* (1970) were critical and popular successes, as was the more recent *Un cœur en hiver* (1993). For Eric Neuhoff the similarity resides in, 'L'amitié. Les bagnoles. Les cinq à sept. Les sourires désabusés. L'espoir malgré tout'[13] (Neuhoff 1992). Alternatively, its obsessive navel-gazing put an English reviewer in mind of 'A French Woody Allen without any jokes!'[14] Kurys' film is in tune with the times to the extent that it expresses concerns about women's roles and the function of the hetero-sexual couple in the postfeminist 1990s. When read in conjunc-tion with *Coup de foudre*, it also bears witness to changes in women's condition between the 1950s and the 1990s. Marriage no longer constitutes the institutional framework against which women have to play out their lives and motherhood has become an option rather than an obligation. But whereas in *Coup de foudre*, the mother's assertion of independence was admirable and rendered possible by female friendship, in *Après l'amour* the modern woman does not always know what to make of her inde-pendence. What really links the two films, then, is the insecurity expressed in the figures of the lonely daughter at the end of *Coup de foudre*, after her parents' love has ended, and the isolated writer of *Après l'amour*, faced with the after-effects of the sexual revol-ution of the 1960s.

References

Errigo, Angie (1993), *Après l'amour*, *Today*, 13 August.

Gonzalez, Claude (1992), 'Isabelle Huppert, Diane Kurys, dix ans de coups de foudre', *Le Figaro Magazine*, 17 April.

13 'Friendship. Cars. Assignations. Cynical smiles. Hope despite everything.'
14 See Angie Errigo (1993).

Heymann, Danièle (1992), 'Le cœur en quarantaine, *Après l'amour*', *Le Monde*, 17 April.

Kurys, Diane (1992), 'Entretien avec Diane Kurys', *Après l'amour*, publicity brochure.

Neuhoff, Eric (1992), '*Après l'amour* de Diane Kurys, les choses de la vie', *Le Figaro Magazine*, 2 May.

Philippe, Claude-Jean (1992), 'Des scènes comme ça, ça ne s'invente pas', *France Soir*, 24 April.

A la folie

Kurys' seventh film shows a return to familiar topics and an interesting if not entirely successful attempt to do something different with that material. *A la folie* reworks the theme of sisters, already explored in *Diabolo menthe* and *La Baule Les Pins*, but focuses this time on their emotional bonds as adults after the death of the mother. In an interview published in the film's publicity brochure (Kurys 1994), Kurys denied, as usual, that the film was based on the facts of her own life, 'J'ai une sœur aînée, mais la ressemblance s'arrête là. Il y a certains détails vrais, mais par petites touches.'[1] At the same time, she acknowledged that the inspiration for the film was autobiographical: 'J'ai une sœur et j'ai souffert d'être la cadette. Nous avons trois ans de différence, je la mettais sur un piédestal et elle en abusait!.'[2] *A la folie* takes to an extreme the complex mixture of desire and resentment felt by the younger sister of *Diabolo menthe* and, arguably, allows her to settle the score with her older sibling. At the same time, the role of the older sister once more calls into question the viability of the heterosexual couple, and the role of the younger sister as a successful conceptual artist allows Kurys' relationship to her own art to be further explored.

Kurys felt ready to take a more experimental approach to

1 'I have an older sister but the resemblance stops there. Certain details are true, but just little touches.'
2 'I have a sister and I suffered from being the younger one. There are three years between us, I put her on a pedestal and she let me down!'

filmmaking with *A la folie* and as a result *A la folie* is more of an exercise in style than her earlier films. The theme of sisters replaying to the point of madness the sado-masochistic games of their childhood was designed as a sort of black comedy which would also function as a psychological thriller through the introduction of suspense to create fear and apprehension. '[J]'avais envie de choquer, de bousculer, de déranger les gens avec ce sujet'[3] (Frois 1994). However, Kurys also wanted at some level to remain within a realist register, 'Il fallait que l'histoire reste réaliste, qu'on se dise, même au moment des scènes les plus dérangeantes: "C'est possible, tout ça aurait pu arriver ..."'[4] (Kurys 1994). Kurys' confused ambitions for the film are reflected in the film's casting. She gave the roles of the sisters, Alice and Elsa, to Anne Parillaud and Béatrice Dalle, two major stars of the 'cinéma du look'. *A la folie* draws on their earlier star images, Parillaud/Nikita the submissive product of patriarchal violence who is also a survivor in *Nikita* (Luc Besson 1990), Dalle/Betty the creature of passions driven to violence and madness in *37°2 le matin/Betty Blue* (Jean-Jacques Beineix 1986). Kurys was originally looking for an intense, physically expressive style for the film, developed through working closely with the actresses, 'Béatrice a agi de manière un peu folle, éclatée, éperdue, avec une certaine ambiguïté, tandis qu'Anne a créé son personnage – à la fois vulnérable et fort – de façon beaucoup plus construite. Toutes deux ont beaucoup apporté'[5] (Levieux 1994). However, she chose the unknown Patrick Aurignac to play Alice's live-in lover and wrote the part of Elsa's husband for comedian Alain Chabat, best known at the time for his presence in the French TV show *Les Nuls*. The mix of actors and acting styles, itself a consequence of the intended mix of film genres, is symptomatic of the film's lack of coherent purpose or style.

3 'I wanted this material to shock people, shake them up and disturb them'.
4 'The story had to remain realistic, so that people would say, even in the most disturbing scenes, "Yes, that could have happened".'
5 'Béatrice acted in a rather mad, explosive, frantic way, and gave the role a certain ambiguity, while Anne constructed her character – who is both strong and vulnerable – in a much more controlled manner. They both contributed a lot.'

The focus on sisters augured well for a Kurys film, given that her most successful films to date, *Diabolo menthe* and *Coup de foudre*, have centred on relationships between girls and women. However, the decision to approach the topic as a realist drama within a genre film framework means that the subtle observations of changing relationships typical of a Kurys film give way to more crudely drawn behaviour and actions. The American title, *Six Days, Six Nights*, emphasises the unusual focus on a relatively short timescale but, like Kurys' other films, *A la folie* depends as much on the ups and downs of interpersonal relationships as on a linear plot. As a result, the thriller element of the film gets in the way of credible characterisation while the awkwardly imposed cyclical ending undermines any dramatic effects produced by the concentrated timespan. However, the mix of genres opens the film up to a reading of the theme of sisters on more than one level. As well as exploring in fiction the relationship between Kurys and her sister, the sisters have a more symbolic function. Like classic melodramas which polarise women into the straight woman and the vamp, the good mother and the bad mother, representations of sisters have often been used to project patriarchal fantasies of 'good' and 'bad' femininity.[6] Such representations normally work to condemn and punish 'the madwoman in the attic' and encourage the spectator to endorse a patriarchal definition of the good, submissive, feminine woman. Many women directors have worked to overturn this polarity, notably the West German director Margarethe von Trotta (in films like *The Sisters* (1979), *The German Sisters* (1981) and *Sheer Madness* (1983)). Although *A la folie* reworks conventional thrillers by marginalising a male point of view and inviting identification with a woman who appears to be liberated rather than submissive, it pits the central female character against a woman whose transgression is even more marked, and treats that transgression with classic (patriarchal) condemnation. Kurys' representation of sisters within a genre framework could have functioned as an interesting device for exploring the split self of the modern, independent woman,

6 See Lucy Fischer (1989).

but instead risks reproducing a stereotypical polarisation between acceptable and unacceptable femininity.

The film opens with a pre-credit sequence which establishes Elsa (Dalle) as a threat to the sanity of Alice (Parillaud), whose artwork forms the backdrop to the credit sequence. Elsa, dressed in a red petticoat, stumbles over children's toys in the dark and settles down for a restless night on the sofa, covered in a man's green mac; the film cuts to the breakfast table, where she treats her uncomprehending husband, Thomas (Chabat), with the contempt he deserves and walks out, still wearing his slippers and mac, to fetch milk from the shop; on impulse she decides not to go back home, and the extra-diegetic song, *Here We Go Again*, sung by Jerryka Souxwell, informs the spectator that Elsa is about to cause trouble. Elsa's lack of respect for convention is confirmed by the insolent, withering look she gives the man on the coach who looks aghast at her as she drinks her milk straight from the carton. The music carries over into the credit sequence which focuses on the hands of an artist lovingly putting the finishing details to some artwork involving blue-coloured sand worked into shapes etched on glass. Like *Coup de foudre*, then, *A la folie* uses an opening parallel sequence to link its two central female characters, one an unhappy wife and mother, the other an artist; this time, however, the relationship is constructed as threatening rather than pleasurable. The hands of the artist (in contrast with the man's hands in the sink at the start of *Après l'amour*) turn out to belong to Alice, whose self-absorbed, introspective existence is trebly threatened in the sequences which follow. First, Sanders, her agent (Bernard Verley), just back from New York, promises her an exhibition, and she runs away from him, thinking she is not yet ready. Then she discovers that her lover, Franck (Aurignac), has moved into her flat without her knowledge or permission, and runs away again, back to Sanders. Then, when Elsa slips her visiting card, a drawing of a dead dog, under Alice's door, just as she and Franck are making love, Alice goes outside to look for her and invites her in. From that moment, Elsa's presence calls into question Alice's already troubled identity as an artist and highlights the fragility of the couple she forms with Franck.

The convoluted plot is primarily concerned with permutations in the relationships between the three main protagonists. Alice thinks she loves both Franck and Elsa, but Franck, who becomes increasingly proprietorial towards Alice, is initially hostile to Elsa, and Elsa, who wants to resume the intimacy with and power over her sister that she had enjoyed as a child, is happy to provoke Franck's antagonism. Alice therefore finds herself caught between them, first expressing affection and concern for her sister, then rejecting her as her relationship with Franck becomes threatened. Thomas' arrival spurs her into protecting Elsa once more and, despite Elsa's provocative behaviour, she comforts her and allows her to take over the bedroom. However, when Alice joins Franck on the sofa, Elsa declares she is leaving, only to step back off the train just when Alice and Franck think she has gone. Thereafter, the relationships between the trio take on a new turn. Franck begins to respond positively to Elsa's provocations, Alice becomes increasingly suspicious of Elsa's behaviour and Elsa thus reasserts power over Alice. When Alice rejects her, she destroys Alice's studio and convinces Franck that it was destroyed by Alice, then she convinces Alice that she is having an affair with Franck, then, when Alice tries to leave, she assists Franck in keeping Alice a prisoner in the flat and seduces Franck, taking Alice's place as his lover. Alice's love for and tolerance of both Elsa and Franck reaches breaking point and, indeed, all three characters reach emotional states bordering on madness (as anticipated by the title). Alice starts to bang her head against the radiator to which she has been tied and, after Franck and Elsa release her, holds a big kitchen knife to Elsa's throat. However, she ignores Franck's advice to take action and hugs her sister before telling her she never wants to see her again. Franck drops the door keys and turns to the bottle and, ignoring Elsa's warning that she will soon be back, Alice runs away, as she did at the beginning of the film, leaving Elsa a lonely figure at the window. The six days and nights come to an end without any dramatic catharsis.

The film could have ended on Alice's emergence into the open spaces of the city at daybreak. Instead it cuts to a final sequence set in New York, where Alice is installed in a new apartment with a new boyfriend, and Sanders arrives to announce that the exhibition of her work is about to take place. Once again, however, a drawing of a dead dog appears under the door, accompanied by the music of 'Here we go again'. The film closes with a medium close-up of Alice staring out of the window, framed by netting, then turning back to look at the camera, her identity yet again under threat. (The shot recalls the freeze-frame of Anne turning back to the camera in *Diabolo menthe*.) There is no final vision of what Alice sees, and she has no words, no voice, to express what she is feeling; the closing image represents her as paralysed, isolated and boxed in. The insistent cyclical structure of the film suggests that she has gained no new self-knowledge and that there is no way out of her predicament. The self which tries to establish a life within the patriarchal world represented by her agent and her lover will continue to be haunted by the self represented by the demonic, abject Elsa. The film offers no possibility of Alice reconciling the different aspects of her life and achieving wholeness, and thereby denies the spectator any satisfying emotional closure.

A la folie is set in Paris in a vague contemporary present which provides even fewer socio-cultural references than *Après l'amour*. Alice, significantly, owes both her living and working spaces to the benevolence of her agent, a surrogate father figure. She has a well-equipped artist's studio and a large attic flat only a short walk away, with a magnificent rooftop view over the Eiffel tower which contrasts with the enclosed space of the flat below. The *mise-en-scène* is an expression of Alice's attempt to compartmentalise and control her work and her relationships (which is even more pronounced than Lola's in *Après l'amour*). But her artwork has already taken over her bedroom and in the course of the narrative both spaces are progressively invaded and destroyed by others. Near the beginning of the film, Alice returns home from her studio to find Franck moving in with all his belongings, including a large Bendix fridge (reminiscent of Michel's fridge in *Coup de foudre*). When Elsa arrives, Alice's studio becomes a site for the playing out of their sado-masochistic relationship, from Elsa's initial touching and commenting on Alice's paintings to the frenzied violence with which she destroys the studio and its contents. Elsa, like Franck, also invades Alice's flat. Disputes about the ownership of clothing and the positioning of furniture and objects, particularly the sofa bed, mark shifts in the power relations between the three characters. Certain objects, like the vase of sunflowers which Franck gives Alice and Elsa smashes in rage at Thomas, acquire rather obvious symbolic resonances. In particular, the wounded pigeon trapped in the netting of the larder, saved by Franck but then kept caged in a crate, seems to represent both Elsa, the wounded creature taken in by Alice, and Alice herself, trapped and caged by Franck and Elsa. The intensity generated by Alice's privileged but claustrophobic spaces and her self-imposed isolation from the rest of the world (apart from her agent) is at odds with the realistic atmosphere of the other briefly glimpsed settings of the film, like the teashop where Thomas' lover works, the gym where Franck works out, the shop and restaurant they visit to celebrate the sale of Alice's painting.

Kurys worked on the design of *A la folie* with the same team as for *Après l'amour*, though to less effect. As Elley argues, 'Fabio Conversi's bright glossy lensing is always a treat for the eye, but it's wrong for a pic supposedly concerned with destructive passions' (Elley 1994). Similarly, the original music scored by Michael Nyman, which Elley describes as 'a treat for the ears', fails to generate the tension and anxiety needed to make the film work as a psychological thriller. Nevertheless, colour and lighting along with other elements of *mise-en-scène* are used in a stylised way to represent differences between the sisters. Alice is associated with blue, Elsa with red, green and shadow. The gamine-like Alice has a short-cropped hairstyle, big eyes and a little girl's voice, and moves in a girlish way. Her simple, neat, often androgynous clothing makes her look childlike and vulnerable (perhaps excessively so for the woman she is) but also sweetly sexy. In contrast, the unkempt Elsa is more sexually mature and has a distinctive husky, sexy voice. Her disturbing appearance and wild behaviour allow her to figure the duplicity and ambivalence of perverse female sexuality. She deliberately plays with the wearing and removal of her reading glasses, she casually and indiscriminately borrows both men's and women's clothing (Thomas' mac and slippers, Franck and Alice's shirts and dressing-gowns), and she manipulates the way she is seen by others by switching provocatively between her outerwear (the mac), and displays of her underwear (particularly her bright red bra, pants and petticoat) and her nakedness. Contrasts in the sisters' artwork also foreground their difference. Alice's otherworldly blue shapes and swirls, described by Elsa as like signs of the cosmos, signify her femininity and sensitivity, but also her withdrawal from the world, while Elsa's two dimensional black and white drawing of a dead dog is crude, morbid and aggressive. The drawing may, as Elsa claims, symbolise how she feels about herself; but when Alice remembers her father saying that, whereas Elsa was beautiful, she, Alice, 'a du chien' ('had got what it takes'), the dead dog comes to figure a projection of Elsa's destructive desire for Alice.

The film ostensibly deals with a threesome but, despite scenes centring on Elsa and/or Franck from which Alice is absent, it is Alice's point of view which the spectator is primarily invited to identify with and Alice who constitutes the object of Elsa's desire. The film invites comparison between the fragile order of Alice's life and the disorder brought about by her fascinating, monstrous sister. The aloof, childless and childlike Alice, who is also a talented, dedicated artist, becomes progressively more passive and introverted as Elsa starts to take over her life. Elsa is a restless, unhappy woman, an artist who settled for marriage and motherhood, an art teacher whose life has failed to live up to her dreams and who walks out on her responsibilities as wife and mother, the only character in Kurys' films to abandon her children (who only appear in the pre-credit sequence).[7] Elsa sets out to entice her sister back into the perverse twilight world of their relationship as children (the film notably fails to consider alternative solutions to Elsa's predicament) and takes refuge in deception and violence, which becomes more and more excessive as Alice fails to satisfy her needs. Her wilful play with masculine and feminine dress codes, her transgression of the boundaries between adult and

7 Kurys affirmed in interview that her experience of motherhood in the 1990s made her less predisposed to identify with children.

childish behaviour, and the knowing combination of feminine wiles and masculine assertiveness that she employs in her seduction of Franck and in her teasing love/hate relationship with Alice, all exemplify the ways in which she is marked as a figure of abjection.

For the narrative to make sense on a realist level, the emotional bonds between the two women need to be convincing, but the film fails to establish the complexity of their family past. In *The German Sisters*, for example, Margarethe von Trotta establishes the relationships between the sisters through the use of flashbacks which provide both family background and a sense of German history. To some extent Kurys' earlier films constitute a background for the sisters of *A la folie,* but the film makes no specific reference to them, even through the names of the characters. Instead, the sisters' past has to be grasped through traces of conversations and memories which do not adequately explain why they should have such intense feelings about one another. Whereas Elsa has remained closely attached to her family, Alice has not seen her father or sister for two years and has not answered Elsa's letters. However, Elsa's probing into her belongings reveals, first, that Alice has been keeping her mother's ashes in an urn at the back of a cupboard and, second, that she has kept all Elsa's letters. The discovery of the mother's ashes in the middle of the night results in a grotesque scene in which, after accusing Alice of not caring about her mother, Elsa scatters the ashes out of the window and they blow back into her face. If Alice has tried, unsuccessfully, to repress her relationship to the family, Elsa here is seen to be too close, the boundary between her self and her mother too thin, her response hysterical and extreme. Such over-identification violates a cultural taboo and marks the abject, grieving Elsa as a threat to patriarchal order. The loss of the mother accounts for the desire for intimacy between the sisters and leads to a moment of tenderness. But the desire to merge with the mother is at odds with the daughters' need for autonomy and accounts for their emotional problems. *A la folie* confirms what was hinted at in *Diabolo menthe*, namely, the elder sister's privileged relationship with the mother and the younger sister's feeling of not being loved. Alice recalls her judgemental, punitive mother catching her shoplifting a nightshirt, walking along the street in front of her repeating, 'Ma fille est une voleuse'[8] (as in *Diabolo menthe*), and forcing her to wear the duly purchased nightshirt every night for the next term. The pain of the memory is only softened by recalling how she and Elsa dressed up their dog in the nightshirt to meet their mother after work. In the past, then, Elsa's presence enabled Alice to endure her mother's rejection of her.

However, Alice is forced to confront the more negative aspects of her relationship with her sister when Elsa challenges her version of events and produces other narratives about the past which work to fix Alice into a state of childlike dependency. Elsa suggests they should go away to Quiberon together because they had fun there as children, so Alice announces that she never liked Quiberon; Elsa reminds Alice that she used to love eating raw pastry, so Alice denies it and walks out of the kitchen. But Elsa's grotesque story of how she gave Alice two helpings of cockroach purée underlines most forcefully how Alice is the loser in the game of memory. Whether Alice denies the truth of the story or claims she had known about it all along, she merely reinforces Elsa's ability to control and torment her, and is unable to turn the story to her own advantage. Elsa's capacity to hurt is repeated with more harmful effects when she deliberately trashes Alice's studio and leaves a condom on the bathroom floor to make Alice think that she has slept with Franck. The extent of her madness can be gauged by the fact that she compares the sequestration of the adult Alice to the sado-masochistic games they played when they were young (like the 'Chinese torture' depicted in *La Baule Les Pins*). Her pathologically regressive behaviour works to suffocate and infantilise Alice and, like the mother, prevent her from achieving autonomy.

The film plays with the psychological thriller genre by hinting that the bond between the sisters may also be a sexual one. At one point in the narrative game, Alice tells Franck that she and Elsa are not sisters but ex-lovers, a notion which Franck scoffs at but

8 'My daughter's a thief.'

which shows Alice to be capable of entertaining incestuous/lesbian fantasies. Subsequently, Franck sees the two women lying naked together on the bed, asleep, before Alice returns to join him on the sofa. Later Elsa attempts to repair relations with her sister by kissing her and telling her she cannot live without her. Alice's rejection of her at that point initiates the cycle of physical violence, which includes scenes of both Franck and Elsa caressing the captive Alice. The possibility of desire between women is also inscribed into the heterosexual lovemaking scripts when Alice asks Franck if he desires Elsa and Elsa gets Franck to describe what Alice does during sex. Though these scenes serve primarily to conjure up male-centred fantasies, they also represent Alice's fear of being taken over by Elsa and Elsa's desire to merge with Alice. The sex scenes are troubling, though, in that, although the women are sexually active, spectators are encouraged to adopt a male point of view through voyeuristic shots of Parillaud's buttocks and Dalle's breasts. There is no attempt to represent lesbian desire from a female point of view, nor is the naked male body displayed as the object of a female gaze. A comparison between the scene in *A la folie* where Elsa examines her breasts in the bath as Alice looks on, and the scene in the changing-room in *Coup de foudre* where Léna and Madeleine look in the mirror and compare breasts, highlights the differences in Kurys' filming of the two sets of women. Whereas the two-shots and exchanges of looks in *Coup de foudre* express the women's tenderness and intimacy, the antagonistic cross-cutting of *A la folie* dramatises the tension between the sisters, which is aggravated by Elsa's selfish appropriation of the bathroom, her narcissism, her aggressive questioning of Alice, and the spectator's awareness of Franck's presence outside the frame. The potent theme of desire between women is transformed into a less transgressive scene of female rivalry.

Even though it is figured negatively, however, the emotional intensity of *A la folie* lies in the relationship between the sisters and not in their relationships with men. As in Kurys' earlier films, *A la folie*'s representation of the heterosexual couple and masculinity is ambiguous and contradictory. The narrative is framed by a sense of the fragility and impermanence of the couple. It is initiated by Elsa's walking out on her life with Thomas and comes to a close with a sequence showing Alice with Franck's replacement, suggesting that the formation and rupture of the couple are part of a repetitive cycle. Though men are represented through two apparently different if equally inadequate male figures, both men (and potentially Franck's replacement too) are actually objects of exchange between the women. Thomas had a relationship with Alice before marrying Elsa, and Elsa takes over Franck, possibly with Alice's connivance, since the film constantly questions whether the couple she forms with Franck is 'the right one'. Each male is desirable enough temporarily to break up the dyad constituted by the sisters, but each is ultimately rejected. In Thomas' case, rejection is attributable to his chronic infidelity (he has been having an affair with Betty the babysitter) and his bumbling insensitivity (as when he fails to communicate with Elsa across the cluttered breakfast table and reveals that he wants his credit cards back as much as he does his wife). In Franck's case, rejection is due to his possessiveness and his inability to accept being just an object of desire. Franck is a self-confident, good-looking, slightly disreputable working-class youth from the *banlieue*, with a career ahead of him as an amateur boxer, whom both women find seductive (though the film does not develop his character enough to suggest why). Kurys cast Aurignac in the part because she liked the combination of sensitivity and muscularity, and Elsa's first comment on meeting Franck is, 'Il est beau!'.[9] However, Franck repeatedly struggles against his objectification without realising that his attempts to impose himself on Alice bode ill for the future of their relationship. His decision to give up boxing because it is not a good occupation for a prospective father is as disturbing for Alice as his moving in with her had been, since motherhood is clearly not on her agenda. His resort to physical violence to prevent Alice from leaving him (he locks her in, hits her and ties her to the radiator) renders their relationship impossible (like Michel's acts of violence in *Coup de foudre* and *La Baule Les Pins*).

9 'He's good-looking!'

He may think he is acting on his own volition when he makes love to Elsa, but he is only a pawn in the psycho-sexual game between the sisters, a fact which he only grasps when Alice refuses to strike Elsa and go away with him. The narrative functions, then, to reduce the principal male character from romantic lead to passive non-entity, and casts doubt on the future of his successor.

If a close relationship with women is a threat to autonomous female identity, and men are insignificant and interchangeable, what is there left? *A la folie* opts yet again for consolation in art, and Alice's doubts and fears about her work and her identity can be seen to mirror Kurys' own preoccupations. In *A la folie*, Alice is on the brink of success in her chosen career. Her first words in the film, 'c'est magnifique, non?',[10] spoken to her agent as she shows him her latest creation, indicate her confidence in her work, even if she protests that she is not yet ready to exhibit. During the course of the film, an article about her work, with accompanying photograph, gets published, an American art collector purchases two of her paintings, and an exhibition is about to be realised. However, Alice's pleasure is blighted by the presence of the critical, bullying older sister who functions as her *alter ego* and voices the doubts she has about the validity of her work.

Elsa argues that Alice's choice of non-figurative motifs indicates her lack of sensitivity to people, and that her limited colour range is a reflection of her limited vision (just as her inability to make sauces is a sign of her limited taste). What is more, since it was Elsa who first taught Alice how to paint with sand on glass, her presence evokes Alice's guilt at having stolen the idea from her sister and her fear that it lacks originality. Arguably, the film summons up the demons which haunt Kurys' feelings about her own work, and there is a lot at stake in Alice's self-justification which turns into an attack on her older sister. Alice accuses Elsa of blighting her life because she lacks the drive to make anything of her own life, and points out that the techniques she uses are available for anyone to exploit and not the exclusive property of her sister. She rounds off the attack by telling her sister that she

10 'it's magnificent, isn't it?'.

cannot love her and walks out on her. The scene is set up as
though Alice needs to defend herself from Elsa, whereas in fact
she is knowingly contributing to Elsa's psychological destruction.
Her speech precipitates Elsa's acts of revenge which begin with
the destruction of the studio and continue with Elsa goading
Franck into sequestrating Alice and taking her place as Franck's
lover. When Alice is released, she has the opportunity to destroy
Elsa physically, but after (unconvincingly) wielding the kitchen
knife, she decides instead, anti-climactically, simply to tell her
sister that she doesn't want to see her again. Her forbearance, her
ability to resume a 'normal' life, and the fact that her exhibition is
expected to go ahead at the end of the film, vindicate her
generosity, resilience and creativity and show that her success has
been achieved against immeasurable (if projected and fantasised)
odds. The film works (or is intended to work) as a justification for
the artist's repression of the (monstrous) feminine influences on
her life, her acceptance of the patriarchal art world on which she
depends, and her solipsistic involvement in her work. But since
the dice have been stacked against Elsa, it is not surprising that at
the end of the film the fears and anxieties invested in the demonic
sister/self resurface.

Arguably, the successful novelist and mother-to-be of *Après
l'amour* has been succeeded by an even more revealing self-
portrait in the representation of the beleaguered artist of *A la folie*
who is confronted with her inability to integrate the 'feminine'
into her life and work. It is surely significant that Alice's non-
representational art makes no contribution to the representation
of women, and that her relationship with another woman artist,
her sister, is confrontational and aggressive. Alice turns to
Sanders for advice on using her love affair to fuel her art (rather
than the mother figure of *Un homme amoureux*) and their
affectionate father–daughter relationship affirms rather than
contests one of French cinema's dominant paradigms.[11] Alice's
anxieties about femininity, projected onto the monstrous figure of
the sister, the fascinating but destructive 'bad' mother and vamp,

11 See Ginette Vincendeau (1992).

mask fears about her autonomy as a female artist and guilt about separating off from her past. The ending pessimistically suggests that Alice's artistic expression, on which she depends for her sense of identity, will be continually at risk from recurring doubts and fears which she is unable to control. The film's final image of the immobilised, silent artist is disconcerting in its denial of a confident, original woman's voice.

References

Elley, Derek (1994), '*Six Days, Six Nights*', *Variety*, 17 October.

Fischer, Lucy (1989), 'Sisters: the divided self' in *Shot/Countershot Fim Traditon and Women's Cinema*, London, Macmillan Education Ltd, 172–215.

Frois, Emmanuelle (1994), '*A la folie*, Diane Kurys ou l'amour vache', *Le Figaro*, 28 September.

Kurys, Diane (1994), *A la folie*, publicity brochure.

Levieux, Michèle (1994), 'Le film de Diane Kurys a du chien', *L'Humanité*, 14 September.

Vincendeau, Ginette (1992), 'Family plots: the father and daughters of French cinema', *Sight & Sound*, 1: 11 (NS), 14–17.

Conclusion: Kurys' authorial signature

The series of interrelated semi-autobiographical films written, directed and produced by Diane Kurys provide a unique source for the analysis of female authorship. Kurys' first seven films transpose and rework the author's memories of the past and anxieties about the present through patterns of characters and situations which recur from film to film. Their focus on a woman's life history and on the family as a formative experience in the construction of identity is of particular interest for spectators of Kurys' generation. Their sympathetic, detailed evocations of 'ordinary' lives in the 1950s and 1960s re-inscribe girls and women into postwar history and provide a critique of women's subordination within marriage. Their depictions of more unconventional women's lives in the films set in the present continue to address issues raised by the social revolution of May 1968 and the feminist movement which followed. At the same time, the incorporation of more stereotypical women's roles in the contemporary films indicate an underlying anxiety about femininity and its significance. The continuities and contradictions of the films provide the basis for identifying Kurys' authorial signature.

I have already argued in the Introduction that this authorial signature is double-voiced, its ambivalence due on the one hand to the need for successful woman directors to find survival strategies within a misogynist French film industry, and on the other to the particularities of Kurys' own formative experiences. Just as Kurys' films both evoke and deny their status as autobiography, Kurys'

authorship is both affirmed and qualified by the way it is presented. From *Diabolo menthe* onwards, each Kurys film is based on
an original screenplay and presented as 'a Diane Kurys film'.
However, the first six films were co-produced by Alexandre Films,
which bears Arcady's name, not hers, and, with the exception of
Diabolo menthe, each of her screenplays has been adapted with the
assistance of a male co-writer (Alain Le Henry, Olivier Schatzky or
Antoine Lacomblez). Although Kurys' route into writing and
directing was that of the actress unhappy with the roles available
to her as a woman, her filmmaking practices remain embedded
within a patriarchal culture. This is even the case with the way
music is used within the films, for Kurys' musical advisors are
male (as are the musicians represented in *Après l'amour*) and the
songs used to comment on the action of the (mostly) female-
centred films are written and in most cases sung by men.

The most significant component of Kurys' authorial signature
is the series of female characters who act as the author's stand-ins.
The Kurys figures may not have the same name from film to film
(though they share Jewish-sounding names like Anne Weber,
Sophie Korski, Jane Steiner, Lola Winter) and, indeed, in the films
about sisters they may be embodied in both characters. But continuities between them are apparent, not just from the films' play
with variations on the family structure, career development and
emotional situation of the central protagonist(s), but also from a
study of the casting, from the unknowns of the first two films to
the star cast of the last five. From Saga Blanchard and Candice
Lefranc as children in *Coup de foudre* and *La Baule Les Pins*, to
Eléonore Klarwein as an adolescent in *Diabolo menthe*, Elise Caron
as an older teenager in *Cocktail Molotov*, Greta Scacchi and Anne
Parillaud as young women in *Un homme amoureux* and *A la folie*,
and Isabelle Huppert as a thirty-something woman in *Après
l'amour*, the physical resemblances between Kurys and her stand-
ins are striking. (Similar continuities can be seen in the series of
progressively more glamorous actresses who incarnate the mother
– Anouk Ferjac, Geneviève Fontanel, Isabelle Huppert, Claudia
Cardinale, Nathalie Baye – and in the more limited series of actors
playing the sister, the father and the (male) lovers.) All the films

involve the Kurys figure to a greater or lesser extent, but the refusal of a fully autobiographical voice means that they often do not fully acknowledge the Kurys figure as their subject.

Whether Kurys' stand-in is located in the past or in the present, as a girl or as a woman, the films have in common triangular structures in which she is torn between, or rejected by, or tries to please pairs of others. In the films about the past, the triangles are formed by her mother and father, her mother and sister, or her mother and her mother's lovers; in the films set in the present, by her own lovers, her lovers and their wives, or her lover and her sister. Two recurrent visual motifs draw attention to the Kurys' figure's problematic positioning: the attempt to please others, or distance herself from others, through art, first through theatrical performances, but later through more solipsistic forms of artistic creation; and scenes of exclusion, which emphasise her unhappiness and solitude. All the films, from *Diabolo menthe* through to *A la folie*, contain images of the Kurys figure, framed against doorways or windows, looking on at others, be it in the crucial scenes of her parents' break-up or in the scenes in which others form a successful couple without her. Yet this situation is not specifically associated with being female, since boys and men also experience exclusion (even if it is not foregrounded with the same intensity). Kurys' vulnerable, rebellious child figures are movingly portrayed, thanks to consistently impressive performances from their child actors; however, her self-controlled, independent adults, who have learnt to suppress their vulnerability, are produced through performances which are often read as 'cold' or 'blank'.

The continuing construction of the Kurys figure through triangular relationships suggests a need to investigate the polarisation between the feminine and the masculine in Kurys' films. Kurys' work has conventionally been associated with the experiences of girls and women and Barbara Quart sums up her themes as: 'initiation, rites of passage, to greater or lesser degree through the eyes of girls or women; and also friendship ...' (Quart 1988: 145). But, as the preceding film analyses have demonstrated, there are notable shifts in the way women are represented in Kurys' films. Kurys' mother–daughter relationships are particularly significant in that such relationships are rarely addressed in dominant French cinema, particularly within a precisely delineated socio-historical setting.[1] In *Diabolo menthe, Coup de foudre* and *La Baule Les Pins*, the mother is represented as a complex figure, independent, attractive, strong-minded and sexually active, but constrained by the circumstances in which she lives. The films sympathise with the daughter who does not feel sufficiently loved, but also explain why the mother is the way she is, without turning her into a monster. However, in *Un homme amoureux* she is projected as the idealised 'good' mother, and in *Cocktail Molotov* and *A la folie* she is thoroughly demonised. A similar shift from realism to stereotyping is to be found in the representations of sisters, while the theme of female bonding becomes a structuring absence in the contemporary films. The complex relationship between the schoolgirl sisters of *Diabolo menthe* and the strengths of female friendship portrayed in *Coup de foudre,* both of which are reprised to some extent in *La Baule Les Pins,* are transformed into the hostile and perverse relationship between sisters of *A la folie.* Even more significantly, the female protagonists of *Un homme amoureux, Après l'amour* and *A la folie,* each of whom is a successful artist, have an ambivalent attitude towards motherhood, show no solidarity with other women and offer no direct critique of patriarchal power relations. Instead, the films emphasise their difference from other women through the construction of secondary female figures, mostly young mothers, who are jealous rivals or crazy hysterics, stereotypical roles which belong more appropriately to a patriarchal cinema. The theme of female bonding, then, is to be found only in the films foregrounding the representation of the mother, and the Kurys figure's sense of being excluded from the mother's love may well account for the anger and hostility towards women and the anxieties about femininity which surface elsewhere.

Kurys' films are also interesting for their exploration of relation-

---

1 The mother–daughter relationship is central to other recent women's films, e.g. *Circuit Carole* (Emmanuelle Cuau 1995) and *Rosine* (Christine Carrière 1995), while Tonie Marshall deliberately incorporates cameo roles in her films for her real-life mother, actress Micheline Presle (e.g. *Pas très catholique,* 1994).

ships between women and men, though men are accorded less subjectivity and agency than the female characters. The father–daughter relationship and relationships between the (heterosexual) couple are represented primarily, but not exclusively, from a female point of view. Following the pattern set up by the mother's expulsion of the father, Kurys' films construct men who are less able to cope than women with their tortuous triangular relationships and boys who have more difficulty in coping with life than girls. Kurys' films thus undermine patriarchal constructions of masculinity through secondary male figures who are often pitiable and always inadequate. Nevertheless, men are represented sympathetically, from the absent but loving father figures of the early films to the array of lovers in the contemporary films. It is not insignificant that in Kurys' last film to date, the father figure returns in the form of the art agent looking after the surrogate daughter's career, whereas the mother figure remains at the level of the repressed. With the exception of *Coup de foudre*, Kurys' women still crave male approval, however unsatisfactory their relationships with individual men and however impossible (and undesirable) the formation of a stable heterosexual couple. Despite Kurys' challenge to conventional representations of masculinity, then, the patriarchal system remains disturbingly intact.

The films' dependence on the construction of sexual difference is surprising, given the crossover of gender traits displayed by the central characters. The men have 'feminine', nurturing characteristics, the independent-minded women are in many ways 'masculine', and both men and women suffer from isolation and lack of love. However, female stereotyping in the contemporary films underlines the fact that the characters most able to combine male and female characteristics are the women in Kurys' stand-in family, and particularly the Kurys stand-in herself. The opening trick shot of *Diabolo menthe*, in which Frédérique's head appears to be attached to Marc's body, does not announce a radical destabilisation of gender, but rather prepares for the suggestion of the later films that only the artist is capable of reconciling gender difference. As both *Après l'amour* and *A la folie* indicate, however, the artist's assumption of her femininity is problematic and troubled.

The films' challenge to conventional heterosexuality is also more apparent than real. Because of the lesbian readings made available by *Coup de foudre*'s theme of female friendship and the hint at desire between girls expressed in *Diabolo menthe*, the theme of desire between women has been attributed to Kurys' films in general. According to Judith Mayne, 'All of Kurys' films are marked by the connection between storytelling and a female bond that wavers between the homosocial and the homoerotic' (Mayne 1990: 126). In fact, Kurys' films are more visibly marked by the representation of heterosexual desire, as is clear from the contrast in *A la folie* between the explicit scenes of heterosexual lovemaking and the unconvincing hints at the sisters' lesbian relationship. However, from *Un homme amoureux* onwards, the heterosexual sex scenes underline anxieties about female authorship by refusing to provide a distinctively female point of view. Though the films' narratives may allow for the expression of female (heterosexual) desire, the sex scenes themselves, however unconventionally filmed, are problematic in their reproduction of masculine points of view and their fetishisation of female body parts.

The *mise-en-scène* of Kurys' films is primarily concerned with reproducing the 'reality' of everyday life, and in particular the authentic sounds and images of Kurys' childhood and adolescence. Arguably, the period films avoid the 'museum aesthetic' of heritage cinema, which privileges the pleasures of repossessing in fantasy the landscapes and artefacts of the nostalgically-remembered past, and work instead to insert female points of view on their particular world. Even if, as Quart argues, their perspective on the period is validated by the recourse to 'surprise autobiography' rather than by any in-depth analysis (Quart 1988: 152), their wider socio-political references allow girls and women, unusually, to be inscribed into postwar French social history. The films' reliance on the pleasures to be found in the well-observed details of individual scenes and small but significant incidents means that, in the most women-centred films, particularly *Diabolo menthe* and *Coup de foudre*, there is a reversal in the hierarchy of images. As Foster argues, 'While her films purport to meet the requirements of dominant cinema, they are rendered with a distinctively female eye' (Foster 1995: 213). In these films, the camera is sensitive to girls and women and the interactions between them, and focuses on female subcultures, be it girls at school or women friends enjoying fashion or coping with housework and parenting. Humour emerges from the ways girls and women share jokes about men and what it is to be female. It is notable that, in contrast, the contemporary films are marked by research into a more stylised use of colour and lighting, and that their lack of interest in female subcultures is accompanied by a similar lack of interest in images of shared, everyday social reality.

Kurys' films address a mainstream audience through Kurys' ability to direct 'well-crafted, intelligent studies of human relationships' (Foster 1995: 213). They are not tightly plotted, classic linear narratives, a form often linked to the notion of the 'masculine' text. But nor do they embrace the radical refusal of classic narrative, often associated with the idea of a 'feminine' text, characteristic of the work of avant-garde women filmmakers like Akerman and Duras. Their focus on characters and relationships within recognisable, realistically constructed times and places means that they are not unsettling, even though their episodic narrative structures, more typical of art cinema than popular cinema, leave spectators with the work of putting the pieces together into a coherent whole. The best films allow a variety of points of view to be articulated and enable spectators to identify sympathetically with a range of characters, male and female. But they are open to the criticism that they cut away from their material too quickly and refuse to address any issue in depth. Consequently, despite generic traces of melodrama and the woman's picture through the use of material based on personal life and the family, they are often not fully centred on their central female protagonists, unlike Hollywood melodramas or 'independent women's films' (or romantic fiction for women). Their examination of interpersonal relationships has something in common with television soap opera, another 'woman's genre', but the viewing pleasures of conventional soaps are denied in those films which choose not to foreground relationships between women.

Kurys' films are personal films which owe a debt to what are often considered 'feminine' modes of expression in their (admittedly fragmentary) incorporation of autobiography, diary and letter formats. The use of a dedication or an afterword in three of the films alerts the spectator to the fact that the film is based on the author's autobiographical experiences, while in three other films, a (fragmented) female voice-over either expresses what the protagonist is writing, be it in a diary or letter or as notes in preparation for writing, or indicates her inner thoughts. Furthermore, the ways in which characters and incidents recur from film to film and are reworked into different stories (though usually under different names) produces a never-ending intertextuality which is also considered typically 'feminine'. At the same time, Kurys' films make use of genres which might be considered 'masculine' – the European art movie, the road movie, the 'film within a film', the psychological thriller – and give them a more 'feminine' inflection by their (partial) centring on a female character, their lack of strong, linear plotting and their problematic, open endings.

The cyclical endings are in fact one of the strongest components of Kurys' authorial signature. Instead of tying up narrative threads (none of the films end unproblematically with the restoration of the family or the heterosexual couple), the cyclical structure suggests that, despite changes, things will carry on much as before. Only the films focusing on the mother offer a linear narrative strand leading to female emancipation, and even then, they stop short of visualising it. The final scene of a Kurys' film is typically a reworking of a scene taken from the beginning of the film, and ends on either a freeze-frame and/or a shot of the Kurys figure and/or an afterword which confirms the film's autobiographical sources. The device could be understood as a way of capturing the realities of everyday existence, with an emphasis on process rather than finality. It could also be linked (problematically) with the notion of women's lives functioning in

cycles. Alternatively, it suggests quite literally that the protagonists of Kurys' films are going round in circles, stuck in what, in
the contemporary films, has become an ahistorical time warp, still
trying unsuccessfully to extricate themselves from the psychological damage inflicted by their childhood. The repetitive narrative
structure of these films thus makes them less empowering for
female audiences than their subject matter centring on a female
character might suggest.

Kurys' authorial signature is typified as much by the ambivalence of the way gender and sexuality is constructed, as by the
representation of relationships from a female point of view. The
recurrence of themes and the circularity of the narrative structures of individual Kurys' films and of the cycle of films overall,
from the relationship between sisters in *Diabolo menthe* to that in
A la folie, are signs of an underlying personal psychodrama which
accounts in part for the reluctance of the contemporary films fully
to assume a woman's voice. However, Kurys' next project, a film
about the relationship between George Sand and Alfred de Musset,
marks a departure from her usual disguised semi-autobiographical subject matter. George Sand's life as a successful writer and
unconventional, independent woman will clearly allow Kurys to
pursue her preoccupation with the difficulties creative women
face trying to reconcile freedom, creativity and love. But it is also
an important topic for women's history,[2] and one which lends
itself to Kurys' talent for period reconstruction. It is to be hoped
that Kurys' decision to dramatise a key episode in another
woman's life story will enable her both to give her filmmaking a
new direction and to rediscover the female audiences who loved
her earlier more women-identified films. Whatever Kurys' future
achievements, however, she has earned a place in the history of
French cinema for her sympathetic treatment of the histories and
desires of girls and women; *Diabolo menthe* and *Coup de foudre* in
particular deserve a permanent place in the canon of European
women's filmmaking.

2 George Sand was the topic of Michèle Rosier's *George qui?* (1973).

References

Foster, Gwendolyn Audrey (1995), *Women Film Directors: An Introductory Bio-Critical Dictionary*, New York, Greenwood Press.

Mayne, Judith (1990), *The Woman at the Keyhole, Feminism and Women's Cinema*, Indiana and Bloomington, Indiana University Press.

Quart, Barbara Koenig (1988), *Women Directors The Emergence of a New Cinema*, Westport, Connecticut and London, Praeger.

Filmography

Table of viewing figures for films directed by Diane Kurys

		Paris–Périphérique	France
1977	*Diabolo menthe*	766,000	2,298,000
1980	*Cocktail Molotov*	106,000	212,000
1983	*Coup de foudre*	460,000	1,310,000
1987	*Un Homme amoureux*	265,000	820,000
1990	*La Baule Les Pins*	221,000	709,000
1992	*Après l'amour*	214,500	528,000
1994	*A la folie*	51,000	115,000

Sources: *Le Film Français*, 2429: 20.11.92; *Ecran Total*, 53: 3.11.94

Diabolo menthe 1977 *(Peppermint Soda)*

101 min., col.
Production Company: Films de l'Alma, Alexandre Films
Executive Producer: Serge Laski
Producer: Armand Barbault
Production Manager: Volker Lemke
Assistant Directors: Daniel Wuhrmann, Josette Barnetche, Alain Le
    Henry
Script: Diane Kurys
Camera: Philippe Rousselot, Christian Backmann, Dominique
    Brenguier
Editing: Joelle van Effenterre, Nelly Meunier, Marie-Dominique
    Fournier

Continuity: Hélène Sebillotte
Sound: Bernard Aubouy, Jean-Louis Ughetto
Music: Yves Simon
Art Direction: Bernard Madelenat, Laurent Janet, Tony Egry
Costumes: Thérèse Ripaud
Make-up: Sophie Landry
Awards: Prix Louis Delluc 1977
Principal actors: Eléonore Klarwein (Anne Weber), Odile Michel (Frédérique Weber), Anouk Ferjac (Mme Weber), Michel Puterflam (M. Weber), Yves Renier (Philippe), Robert Rimbaud (M. Cazeau), Marie-Véronique Maurin (Muriel Cazeau), Corinne Dacla (Pascale), Coralie Clément (Perrine Jacquet), Valérie Stano (Martine Dubreuil), Darius Depoléon (Marc).

Cocktail Molotov 1980

100 min., col.
Production Company: Alexandre Films, Antenne 2
Production Manager: Charlotte Fraisse
Assistant Directors: Daniel Whurmann, Patrick Halpine
Script: Diane Kurys with Philippe Adrien, Alain Le Henry
Camera: Philippe Rousselot, Dominique Brenguier
Editing: Joelle van Effenterre, Nelly Meunier
Continuity: Many Barthod
Sound: Bernard Aubouy, Antoine Olivier
Music: Yves Simon
Art Direction: Hilton McConico, Tony Egry
Make-up: Eric Muller
Costumes: Thérèse Ripaud, Dominique Oliva
Principal actors: Elise Caron (Anne), Philippe Lebas (Fred), François Cluzet (Bruno), Geneviève Fontanel (the mother), Henri Garçon (the stepfather), Michel Puterflam (the father), Malène Sveinbjorns-son (the sister).

Coup de foudre 1983 (At First Sight (UK))/(Entre nous (US))

111 min., col.
Production Company: Partner's Production, Alexandre Films, Hachette Première et Cie, Films A2, Société Française de Production de Cinéma
Executive Producer: Ariel Zeitoun
Production Manager: Michel Frichet

Assistant Directors: Emmanuel Gust, Claudine Taulère, Hubert Ennamare, Marie Fernandez, Ofer Lelouch, Fabienne Bichet, Lucile Christol, Périclès Prokopiadis

Script: Diane Kurys

Adaptation: Diane Kurys, Alain Le Henry

Camera: Bernard Lutic

Editing: Joelle van Effenterre

Sound: Harald Maury, Claude Villand, Alix Comte, Gérard Lecas, Dominique Duchatelle

Music: Luis Enriquez Bacalov

Art Direction: Jacques Bufnoir

Costume Designer: Mic Cheminal

Costumes: Anne-Marie Veinstein and René Miguel

Make-up: Jean-Pierre Eychenne, Joël Lavau, Pierre Vad, Maryse Faure, Anne Bourdiol, Jacques Michel

Principal actors: Miou-Miou (Madeleine), Isabelle Huppert (Léna), Guy Marchand (Michel), Jean-Pierre Bacri (Costa), Robin Renucci (Raymond), Patrick Bauchau (Carlier), Patricia Champagne (Florence), Saga Blanchard (Sophie), Guillaume Le Guellec (René).

Un homme amoureux 1987 (*A Man In Love*)

117 min., col.

Production Company: Alexandre Films, Camera One, J.M.S. Films

Executive Producer: Michel Seydoux

Associate Producers (Italy): Marjorie Israel, Armand Barbault

Line Producer: Roberto Guissani

Producers: Michel Seydoux, Diane Kurys

Production Manager: Bertrand van Effenterre

Assistant Directors: Parlo Barzman, Pericles Prokopiadis

Script: Diane Kurys

Adaptation: Diane Kurys, Olivier Schatzky

Camera: Bernard Zitzermann

Editing: Joelle van Effenterre

Continuity: Claudine Taulère

Sound: Bernard Bats

Music: Georges Delerue

Art Direction: Dean Tavoularis

Costumes: Brigitte Nierhaus

Make-up: Joël Lavau

Principal actors: Greta Scacchi (Jane), Peter Coyote (Steve), Peter

Riegert (Michael), Claudia Cardinale (Julia), John Berry (Harry), Jamie Lee Curtis (Susan), Jean Pigozzi (Pizani).

La Baule Les Pins 1990 *(C'est la vie)*

97 min., col.
Production Company: Alexandre Films, S.G.G.C., Films A2
Executive Producer: Robert Benmussa
Producer: Alexandre Arcady
Associate Producer: Jean-Bernard Fetoux
Production Manager: Philippe Lièvre
Assistant Directors: Marc Angelo, Serge Boutleroff
Script: Diane Kurys, Alain le Henry
Camera: Guiseppe Lanci, Fabio Conversi
Editing: Raymonde Guyot
Continuity: Aruna Villiers
Sound: Bernard Bats, François Groult
Music: Philippe Sarde
Art Direction: Tony Egry
Costumes: Caroline de Vivaise
Make-up: Marie-Hélène Duguet
Principal actors: Nathalie Baye (Léna), Richard Berry (Michel), Jean-Pierre Bacri (Léon), Zabou (Bella), Valéria Bruni-Tedeschi (Odette), Didier Bénureau (Ruffier), Julie Bataille (Frédérique), Candice Lefranc (Sophie), Alexis Derlon (Daniel), Emmanuelle le Boidron (Suzanne), Maxime Boidron (René), Benjamin Sacks (Titi).

Après l'amour 1992 *(Love After Love)*

Year of production: 1991
104 min., col.
Production Company: Alexandre Films, TF1 Films, Prodeve
Executive Producer: Robert Benmussa
Producers: Alexandre Arcady, Jean-Bernard Fetoux with Philippe Lièvre
Production Manager: François d'Artemare
Script: Diane Kurys and Antoine Lacomblez
Camera: Fabio Conversi
Editing: Hervé Schneid
Continuity: Claudine Taulère
Sound: Bernard Bats, Claude Villand, Bernard Le Roux
Music: Yves Simon

Art Direction: Tony Egry
Costumes: Mic Cheminal
Make-up: Paul Le Marinel
Principal actors: Isabelle Huppert (Lola), Bernard Giraudeau (David), Hippolyte Girardot (Tom), Judith Reval (Rachel), Yvan Attal (Romain), Lio (Marianne), Laure Killing (Elisabeth), Ingrid Held (Anne).

A la folie 1994 (*Six Days, Six Nights*)

Year of production: 1993
96 min. col.
Production Company: Passion & Production, New Light Films, France 3 Cinéma
Executive Producer: Robert Benmussa
Producer: Alexandre Arcady
Production Manager: Philippe Lièvre
Assistant Director: Marc Angelo
Script: Diane Kurys and Antoine Lacomblez
Camera: Fabio Conversi
Editing: Luc Barnier
Continuity: Véronique Lagrange
Sound (Dolby): Pierre Befve, Claude Villand
Music: Michael Nyman
Art Direction: Tony Egry
Works on glass: Bernard Moninot
Costumes: Mic Cheminal
Make-up: Didier Lavergne
Principal actors: Anne Parillaud (Alice), Béatrice Dalle (Elsa), Patrick Aurignac (Franck), Alain Chabat (Thomas), Bernard Verley (Sanders).

Select bibliography

Diane Kurys

Colvile, G., 'Mais qu'est-ce qu'elles voient? Regards de Françaises à la caméra', *The French Review*, 67: 1, 73–81. A survey of how French women's filmmaking has constructed the male as the object of a heterosexual female gaze, including references to Kurys' films.

Foster, G. A., *Women Film Directors: An Introductory Bio-Critical Dictionary*, Westport, Connecticut and London, Greenwood Press, 1995, 211–13. A succinct summary of Kurys' film career up to *Après l'amour*.

Manceaux, M., 'Diane Kurys: mon aventure-cinéma', *Marie Claire*, June 1983. A key interview in which Kurys discusses her attitudes towards women.

Mayne, J., 'Mistresses of Discrepancy' in *The Woman at the Keyhole: Feminism and Women's Cinema*, Indiana and Bloomington, Indiana University Press, 1990, 124–54. A discussion of self-representation and desire between women as factors in the authorial signatures of certain key European women directors, with brief reference to Kurys.

Quart, B. K., *Women Directors: The Emergence of a New Cinema*, Westport, Connecticut and London, Praeger, 1988, 145–53. A detailed, sensitive and nuanced analysis of Kurys' films up to *A Man in Love*, within a chapter on other key Western European women directors.

Portuges, C., 'Seeing subjects: women directors and cinematic autobiography' in Brodzki, B. and Schenck, C. (eds), *Life/Lines: Theorizing Women's Autobiography*, Ithaca and London, Cornell University Press, 1988, 338–50. A rare essay on women, gender and cinematic autobiography, focusing on European women filmmakers, including Kurys.

Tarr, C., 'Changing representations of women in the cinema of Diane Kurys', *Women in French Studies* 5, 1988. A critique of Kurys' construction of femininity in *Après l'amour* and *A la folie* compared with that of *Diabolo menthe* and *Coup de foudre*.

Tarr, C., 'Heritage, nostalgia and the woman's film: the case of Diane Kurys' in Sue Harris and Elizabeth Ezra (eds), *Visual Culture and French National Identity*, forthcoming. An analysis of how Kurys' four films set in the past challenge the expectations of heritage cinema by introducing a female perspective on postwar French society.

Vincendeau, G., 'Like eating a lot of madeleines', *Monthly Film Bulletin*, 58, 686: 69–70. A revealing interview with Kurys in which she sets out her ideas on women's cinema.

Coup de foudre

Holmlund, C., 'When is a lesbian not a lesbian?: the lesbian continuum and the mainstream femme film', *Camera Obscura* 25/26, 1991, 144–79. An examination of the aesthetic strategies employed in four films which allow for both heterosexual and lesbian responses/identifications.

Kael, P., 'The current cinema, *Entre nous*', New York Times, March 1984, 130, 133–4. A corrective critical view of *Coup de foudre*, highlighting the film's contradictory messages.

Pally, M., 'Extract from *World of our Mothers*', *Film Comment* 20, 1984, 11–17. A juxtaposition of interviews with three women filmmakers with Jewish parents, including Kurys on the background to *Entre Nous/Coup de foudre*.

Powrie, P., '*Coup de foudre*: nostalgia and lesbianism' in *French Cinema in the 1980s*, Oxford, Oxford University Press, 1988, 62–74. A close textual analysis of the film which emphasises its representation of a crisis in masculinity.

Quart, B., '*Entre nous*, a question of silence', *Cineaste*, 1984, 13: 3, 45–7. A comparison of two European films focusing on bonds between women.

Straayer, C., '*Voyage en douce, Entre nous*: the hypothetical lesbian heroine', *Jump Cut* 35, 1990, 50–7. A psychoanalytical approach to two French films which examines how films allow for multiple overlapping readings, and so provide pleasures for lesbian spectators.

Women filmmakers in France

Audé, F., *Ciné-modèles cinéma d'elles*, Lausanne, L'Age d'homme, 1981. An important critical history of women's filmmaking in France to 1980.

Austin, G., 'Women film-makers in France' in *Contemporary French Cinema: An Introduction*, Manchester and New York, Manchester University Press, 1996, 81–98. A good summary of the work of selected contemporary filmmakers, including Kurys.

Breton, E., *Femmes d'images,* Paris, Editions Messidor, 1984. A well-illustrated but highly selective approach to women's filmmaking up to 1983.

Flitterman-Lewis, S., *To Desire Differently: Feminism and the French Cinema*, Urbana and Chicago, University of Illinois Press, 1990. A major *auteur* study of Germaine Dulac, Marie Epstein and Agnès Varda, preceded by a discussion of 'the theoretical issues surrounding the representation of women and the cinematic apparatus'.

Forbes, J., 'Women film makers in France' in *The Cinema in France: After the New Wave*, Basingstoke and London, Macmillan, 1992, 76–102. Grounds women's filmmaking within feminist theory and the women's movement in France, but focuses primarily on Marguerite Duras and Agnès Varda.

Hayward, S., *French National Cinema*, London and New York, Routledge, 1993. An essential background reader on French cinema, with reference to contemporary women filmmakers within the section on 'The age of the postmodern 1958–91'.

Lejeune, P., *Le Cinéma des femmes,* Paris, Editions Atlas Lherminier, 1985. A useful reference work, giving details of 105 French women filmmakers up to 1985 (including Kurys).

Martineau, M., (ed.) *Le Cinéma au féminisme, CinémAction* 9, Autumn 1979. A key issue of *CinémAction* on feminism and cinema which assembles a wide diversity of texts. *CinémAction* did not produce a follow-up until 1993, with G. Vincendeau and B. Reynaud (eds) *20 ans de théories féministes sur le cinéma, CinémAction* 67.

Siclier, J., 'Filmer au féminin' and 'Du côté des femmes' in *Le Cinéma français, 2. De Baisers volés aux Nuits fauves*, Paris, Editions Ramsay, 1993, 45–58 and 189–205. Siclier is one of the rare French cinema historians to give serious consideration to women's filmmaking practices. He devotes a chapter each to women's filmmaking in the 1970s and the 1980s.

Vincendeau, G., 'Women's cinema, film theory and feminism in France', Glasgow, *Screen*, 28: 4, 4–18. An analysis of the problematic relationship between women's filmmaking, the film industry and (the lack of) feminist theory in France, together with a survey of the work of young French women filmmakers.

Women in France

Duchen, C., *Feminism in France From May '68 to Mitterrand*, London, Boston and Henley, Routledge & Kegan Paul, 1986. A lucid account of different feminist practices in France, 'clarifying the divergent political stances and the feminist theory which informs them'.

Duchen, C., *Women's Rights and Women's Lives in France 1944–1968*, London and New York, Routledge, 1994. An exploration of women's everyday lives and competing definitions of femininity in postwar France.

Holmes, D., 'Women in French society 1958–94' in *French Women's Writing 1848–1994*, London & Atlantic Highlands, NJ, Athlone, 1996. A succinct summary of key issues affecting women's lives, as the background to a study of contemporary women writers.

Laubier, C., *The Condition of Women in France: 1945 to the Present*, London and New York, Routledge, 1990. Useful background information and documentation, up to 1990.

Index

Note: page numbers in *italic* refer to illustrations.